THE ENDGAME

ABOUT THE AUTHORS

TOMOKO OGAWA

was born in 1951 in Nagoya.   In 1965, at the age of fourteen, she won the Women's Amateur Honinbo Tournament, which led the following year to her entrance into the Kitani Go School in Tokyo.   There she became a professional go player.   Her promotion record is:

Shodan	1970
2 dan	1971
3 dan	1974
4 dan	1975

In 1975 she scored an impressive 18 wins, 7 losses in professional competition and was named the outstanding woman player of the year by *Kido* magazine.   She is also known abroad, having made go-playing visits to China and Europe.

JAMES DAVIES

was born in 1945 in Philadelphia.   He studied mathematics at Oberlin College and the University of Washington, but came to Japan in 1970 to play go and, as it turned out, to write and translate a large number of go books.   Among those he has written are three other volumes of this series:

Life and Death
Tesuji
38 Basic Joseki (with Kiyoshi Kosugi)

He is also a regular contributor to *Go Review* magazine.

Elementary Go Series, Vol. 6

THE ENDGAME

by
Tomoko Ogawa, 4 dan
and
James Davies

THE ISHI PRESS, INC.

Tokyo

Published by
The Ishi Press, Inc.
CPO Box 2126
Tokyo, Japan

First Printing September 1976
Second Printing September 1982
Third Printing April 1990
Printed in Japan
by Sokosha Printing Co., Ltd.

PREFACE

In this book we have tried to do two things: to cover the basic moves and principles of the endgame; and to show how they are applied in actual game situations. Go is an intellectual pursuit, so we assume that you will want to try to think through as much as you can on your own, and not just take our word for it that such-and-such is a correct move. Accordingly, more than half of the following pages are given over to problems. Working them out may require some patience, but it should make you stronger in a very tangible way.

The primary responsibility for the five chapters is divided as follows.

Chapter 1	Ogawa
Chapter 2	Davies
Chapter 3	Davies
Chapter 4	Ogawa
Chapter 5	Ogawa

We consulted, however, throughout the book. One of us (Davies) drafted the entire text, and the other of us (Ogawa) passed judgement on all the diagrams.

Our thanks go to the Nihon Kiin for the use of their facilities while working on this book, and to James Kerwin, who proofread the manuscript and suggested a number of modifications.

Tokyo, Japan
June, 1976

Tomoko Ogawa
James Davies

TABLE OF CONTENTS

CHAPTER 1

Introducing the Endgame

The endgame could be called the small-scale stage of the game of go. During the opening and middle game the board is open and the fighting tends to range all up and down and across it. By the endgame the board has been more or less divided up into separate territories, and most of the fighting tends to affect only two of them, occurring at a mutual boundary. The opening and middle game are much like a single large battle between two armies; the endgame is like a number of smaller battles going on in different places simultaneously. In a way this makes the endgame easier, because the local engagements, being smaller, are easier to read out, but in a way it makes it harder because one's attention must be focused on several areas simultaneously.

Whether you find it easy or hard, one thing can be said about the endgame: it is decisive because it comes last. True, there is sometimes no endgame—one player loses a large group of stones and resigns early—but in all other cases the endgame determines the victor. Reversals of the lead are frequent. Watch a professional game: you will see the players most tense and serious during the endgame. The endgame may be less exciting than the middle game, but there is a great amount of satisfaction to be gotten from playing it well, no small part of which comes from winning.

It is not surprising that strong professional players are generally strong in the endgame. Sakata, 9-dan, is a brilliant endgame player. Rin, 9-dan, is noted for his ability to squeeze the last drop of profit from an endgame situation. Ishida, 9-dan, considers his greatest strength to lie in the endgame. It would be hard to find any professional or strong amateur who was really weak in the endgame.

What makes for strength in the endgame? One's reading ability and one's eye for tesuji are important, just as they are in the middle game. Another factor is one's ability to count and determine the relative sizes of different moves. These tactical matters, however, are not everything. More important than counting to find the biggest move, for example, is finding ways to make profit in sente, or to keep the enemy from doing so. A player who could not count at all, but understood the difference between sente and gote, would have the advantage over an opponent suffering from the reverse affliction. Knowing whether you are ahead or behind in the game and varying your strategy accordingly is also important. So is making sure that you are always looking at the whole board, not focusing your attention on one part of it and forgetting the rest, as so many amateurs seem to do.

Perhaps the best way to explain the kind of thinking that goes into the endgame is to take you through an actual game and show you directly, and that is what this chapter will do. The game is a professional one, so as we go through it you will see how professionals count, and get lots of glimpses of professional strategy, intuition, and reading in action. Unfortunately, we cannot avoid exposing you to the difficulties and messy details of the endgame, too, but perhaps that is just as well. It is by mastering such difficulties and details that one becomes stronger.

As you proceed through the chapter, you will find some material set aside in boxes. Most of these boxes contain analyses that support statements made in the text, and they can be skipped over without breaking the continuity of the chapter. We recommend that you do skip over them on your first reading and go back to them later, perhaps after finishing chapter 2. Several of the boxes show how the values of certain moves can be counted, and this general method of counting will be explained fully in chapter 2.

The game, which begins on the next page, was my (Ogawa's) third game in the 1971 Oteai (the professional ranking tournament). My opponent, who had the white stones, was Haruo Kamimura, and at the time we were both shodan. Both of us had our eyes on promotions that year, so as you will see, we played very hard. The conditions were six hours per player and no komi. Kamimura, who is now 5-dan, is quite strong. I had a rematch against him recently and lost.

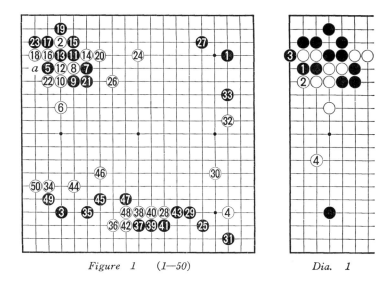

Figure 1   *(1—50)*   *Dia. 1*

Figure 1 shows the first fifty moves, and as you can see, my opponent concentrated on building up a large territorial framework on the left side and in the center, giving me all four corners. By the end of the figure, the weakness of the white group on the lower side had become the important factor in the game.

Looking back at the upper left corner, I wonder if you would have been able to resist the temptation to capture at *a*, instead of playing White 24 or Black 25. This is precisely the sort of move that can and should be saved for the endgame. Suppose Black plays 1 and 3 in Dia. 1, instead of 25 in the figure. Her two-stone capture is certainly big, but the corner was alive even without it and White 4, as compared with a black play in that direction, is big too. Moves like Black 1 and 3, that do not attack or defend but just take profit, are not very attractive during the opening and middle game.

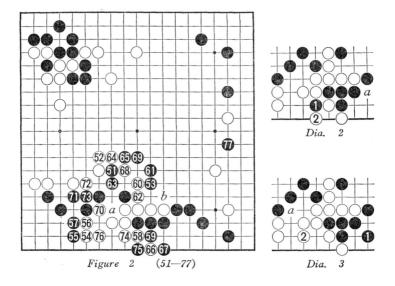

Figure 2   (51—77)

Dia. 2

Dia. 3

I attacked White's weak group with 53, and he spent the next twenty moves or so defending it.   White 66, to point out just one stone in this sequence, was a well-timed forcing play.   If I answered it by giving atari at 1 in Dia. 2, White would play 2, and if I lost this ko, I would stand to lose four more stones to White *a*.   If I played safe by answering at 1 in Dia. 3, however, then after forcing me with *a* in sente (as he did at 70 in the figure), White could connect at 2 to get a living shape. I rejected these two diagrams and answered White 66 at 67, but that made 74 sente, so White was able to live by playing 74 and 76.

He was not absolutely alive, because I could still force a ko with *a*, but he had so many ko threats to escape, starting with *b*, that the ko was not practical yet.   What I had to do now was invade his thin position on the right side with Black 77 and wait for a chance to start the ko later.

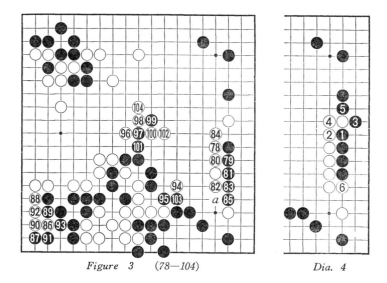

Figure 3   *(78—104)*   *Dia. 4*

Invading the right side with 77 to 85 was extremely large; a fair amount of what might have been white territory was now black territory. Moves like these, that transfer territory from one player to the other, are twice as valuable as moves that just reduce enemy territory or just enlarge friendly territory.

At Black 83 I could have linked up to the upper right with 1, 3, and 5 in Dia. 4. It is hard to say which is better, Dia. 4 or the figure, but Dia. 4 would leave White a big move at 6. If White had answered Black 83 at *a*, then I would have carried out Dia. 4.

After whittling down the lower left corner in sente White exchanged 94 for 95, advanced to 96, bent around me at 98, and cut at 100, forcing me to connect at 103. Black 95 and 103 occupied neutral points, while White 94 (not to mention White 98, 100, etc.) was in a useful position for making territory, but I had compensation in that White had lost most of his ko threats, so the ko on the lower side was now a serious matter.

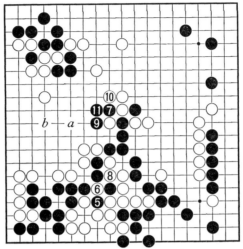

Figure 4   (*105—111*)

White could not afford to lose this ko, so he ignored my first ko threat and captured at 8. The exchange in this figure marked the close of the middle game, and while my opponent was thinking over the first move of the endgame, I surveyed the board and made a rough count of the territories to see who was ahead. This is something that professionals do again and again throughout the course of a game, even in the opening, and I would like to show you how we do it.

The black territory in the lower right was already pretty well settled, so I could get an exact figure for it. First I had to make some assumptions about what its final boundaries would be. I had to assume that eventually White would be able to play 1 in Dia. 5 on the next page in sente; if I did not answer at 2, he could slide all the way in to *a*. Similarly, I had to assume White 3 and Black 4. To complete the boundary on the right edge I put in White ⬡ and Black ⬢. Note that I mentally added equal numbers of black and white stones.

— 14 —

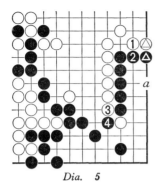

Dia. 5

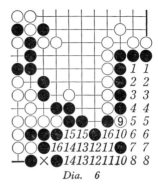

Dia. 6

Next I counted the amount of territory left. I can do this accurately in under five seconds by counting pairs of points, as in Dia. 6. There is a neat column of 8 pairs going down the right edge, two points for the white prisoner at 9, a pair at 10, four more pairs going across the bottom edge at 11 to 14, a pair above them at 15, and finally a pair left over at 16. That makes 32 points, and adding on a point for the stone I captured at ×, I saw that I had 33 points here.

Taking the rest of my territories, I estimated the lower left corner at a glance as 5 points. I estimated the upper left corner pessimistically as 10 points, and the upper right corner optimistically as 15 points. That gave me $33+5+10+15=63$ points of secure territory.

Now why don't you try estimating White's territory? Assume Black a and White b on the left side, and don't count anything for him in the neutral area in the lower right center. See if you don't agree with me that even with the next move, it is hard for White to get 60 points overall, and so my prospects in the game right now were good.

Speaking of White's next move, can you guess what it was before you turn the page?

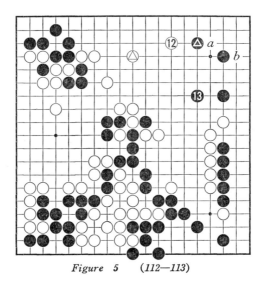

Figure 5 (*112—113*)

White started the endgame with 12, the largest move since besides seizing the open space between the two marked stones on the upper side, it threatened to invade the upper right corner. I knew from experience that my three-stone formation was vulnerable at either *a* or *b*, so after recounting to make sure that it would preserve my lead, I defended with Black 13. White had thus kept sente and could proceed to the next largest point. Can you guess where it was?

The six diagrams at the top of the next page show what could have happened if I had not defended with Black 13. Given the continuation shown, White 1 in Dia. 7 is the most damaging invasion. It may be possible to kill this invasion by descending at 4 in Dia. 8, but Black runs a risk in trying to do so because of the cutting points at *a* and *b*.

In any case, if White is afraid of Black 4 in Dia. 8, he can fall back on White 1 in Dias. 9 to 12. That invasion is unstoppable.

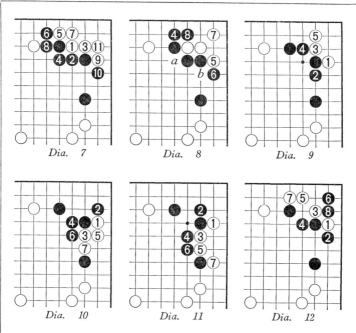

Dia. 7 *Dia.* 8 *Dia.* 9

Dia. 10 *Dia.* 11 *Dia.* 12

With Black 13 on the board, (● in the two diagrams below), White's invasions no longer work. He is unconditionally dead in Dia. 13 (*a* and *b* are miai), and also in Dia. 14, where Black ● makes Black 4 possible.

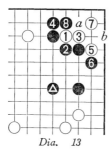

Dia. 13

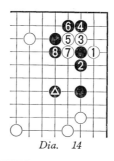

Dia. 14

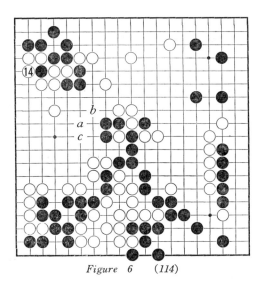

Figure 6   (114)

The time had come to capture at 14.   In terms of the left edge alone, this move was worth sixteen points, as is shown on the next page, and it gave White additional profit on the upper edge by making White 1 in Dia. 15 sente.   If Black fails to answer at 2 and 4, White 4 kills her.   Compare Dia. 15 with Dia. 16; the difference is large.   Since, after 14, White gets to play Dia. 15 free, without giving up his turn, it should be considered a part of the value of White 14, which thus rises from sixteen points to well over twenty points.

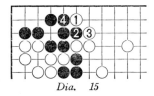

Dia.   15

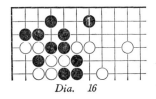

Dia.   16

It may look tempting to play White 14 in the center. The trouble with that was that if White played 14 at *a* in the figure, Black could still move toward her three abandoned stones with *b*. If White played 14 at *b*, however, Black could jump to the left at *c*. White, therefore, would really need two moves to defend this area, while he needed only one at 14.

Here is how the figure sixteen points for the value of White 14 on the left edge was arrived at. Suppose for comparison that Black plays 1 in Dia. 17. That is big in itself, and next she can push out at *a* to reduce White's territory further, as in Dia. 18. White cannot block Black 1 in Dia. 18 directly at 3, or Black cuts at 2, leading to a bad ko for White. Black 1 to 5 in Dia. 18 are sente, so they should be counted as part of Black's profit in Dia. 17.

Similarly, given 14 in the figure, White can play 1 and 3 in Dia. 19 later in sente, and they should be counted as part of his profit. To find the value of White 14, then, what one does is to compare Dias. 18 and 19. In Dia. 18 Black's territory is seven points larger than in Dia. 19: three pairs and the point marked ×. In Dia. 19, White's territory is nine points larger than in Dia. 18: four pairs and the point marked ×. The total difference is 7+9=16 points.

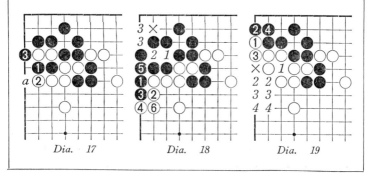

Dia. 17   Dia. 18   Dia. 19

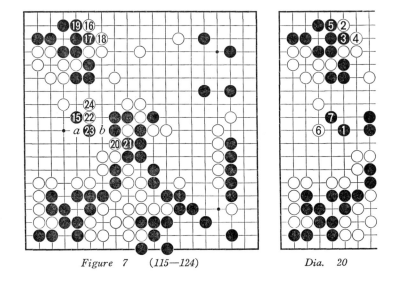

Figure 7 (115—124)   Dia. 20

Now I had sente and could take my pick of the big points left on the board. I chose the two-point jump to Black 15, and before answering it, White made his sente moves at 16 and 18. They were very big, and if he did not make them at once, I might emerge from the fighting in the center with sente and play on the upper side before him.

Next White came up with a counterattack at 20 and 22 that I think must have caught me by surprise. White 24 left *a* and *b* as miai, so Black 15 was going to get cut off. Looking back, I don't know why I didn't play 1 in Dia. 20 instead of Black 15. I must have had some reason for rejecting it, but I do not remember what it was.

Returning to the figure, how would you connect after White 24? Black *a* would not be good, letting White cut off everything with *b*, but would you play *b*, or make a diagonal connection at the point above or below it? Think about this before you read on.

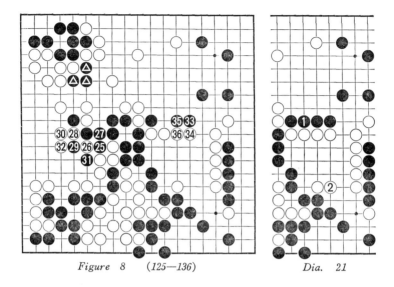

Figure 8   (125—136)   Dia. 21

Black 25 was the right way to connect.   Although White immediately
gave atari at 26 and forced me to fill at 27, the 25–26 exchange was
important in reducing his liberties.

White's counterattack, however, had been a success; with 32 he had
defended both the area on the left and the area around the three stones
marked ⓐ.   Before making my next move, I counted the territories
again.   For myself I got: 33 (lower right)+5 (lower left)+10 (upper
left)+20 (upper right) +2 (prisoners taken in the center)=70.   For
White I got about 60 (left and upper sides)+10 (lower side)=70.   We
were exactly even; for the remainder of the endgame, both of us would
be going all out.

Black 33 and 35 were forcing moves that aimed at attacking the white
group in the lower right, but I stopped short of actually cutting it off
with 1 in Dia. 21, which would just provoke White into living and
making territory with 2, while gaining nothing in return.   Next I went
back to the area around 25–32.   I had a very large move left there.
Can you see what it was before turning the page?

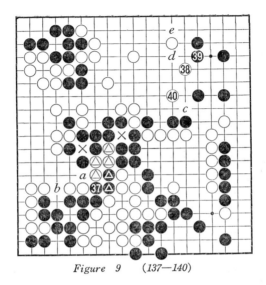

Figure 9   *(137—140)*

Black 37 took the two stones marked ▲ out of atari and captured
the four stones marked ◯. White could not connect at *a*; Black *b*
would answer that. The value of Black 37, as compared with a white
play there, was fourteen points: two points for each of the six stones
captured or liberated, and another pair because the points marked
× were now real territory for me instead of being false eyes. Another
way of looking at it is that my territory had gone up by ten points
(the ◯'s and the ×'s), while White's had gone down by four (the
▲'s).

White 38 and 40, however, gave White about equal compensation,
so the game was still neck-and-neck. I probably considered playing
38 myself instead of 37, as in Dia. 22 on the facing page. Next I
could play *a* in that diagram in sente and make some profit in the
center, but there is something more satisfying in a move like Black
37 in the figure, that gives you fourteen points of solid cash in the
pocket, than in a move like Black 1 in Dia. 22, that may give you
about the same amount, but is comparatively vague.

White 38 threatened an invasion of the upper right corner again, so I defended at 39. White 40 threatened White *c*, which would cut off my three stones in the center. Both White 38 and 40 put very effective pressure on my weak points, forcing me to defend, and thus made profit in sente.

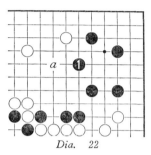

Dia. 22

To return to Black 39, this was the correct defensive move. If Black tries to defend at 1 in Dia. 23, White has the hitting-under tesuji at 2. Black cannot very well capture White 2 with 3, because then White breaks through her defenses with 4, 6, and 8. She has to defend at 3 in Dia. 24, but then White can draw back to 4, leaving the threat of White *a* in the corner. White *a* is White 1 in Dia. 25. If Black descends to 2, White can live in ko with 3, 5, and 7. Black 39 in the figure prevented White 2 in Dias. 23 and 24, and at the same time threatened similar contact plays at *d* or *e* against the white stone.

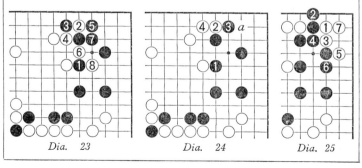

Dia. 23   *Dia.* 24   *Dia.* 25

— 23 —

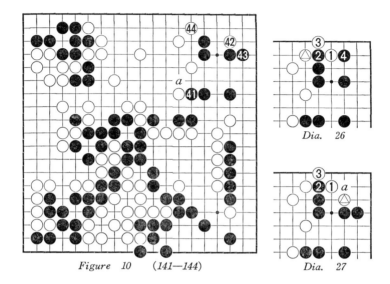

Figure 10 (141—144)

Dia. 26

Dia. 27

I played 41, which stopped the cut and threatened a hane at *a*, but White ignored my move and probed at the corner with 42. Since I answered at 43, the effect of White 42 was to increase the value of White 44. That may be obvious without any diagrams, but let's look at a few anyway.

Suppose White plays ◯ in Dia. 26 without first probing in the corner, and I ignore him. Next he can jump in to 1, but I can stop him with 2 and 4 and hold the damage to reasonable proportions. In Dia. 27, by contrast, with the stone marked ◯ in place, I cannot play Black 4 at *a*.

Similarly, if White plays 1 in Dia. 28 on the next page I can block him at 2, and without the probe, whether or not he can continue at *a* is a bit problematical. In Dia. 29, however, after the same 1 and 2 there is no arguing with White 3.

A good probing move like White 42 in the figure opens up weaknesses in the enemy's position no matter how he replies. Instead of Black 43, I could have played Black 1 in Dia. 30, but that would have left White such possibilities as 2 to 6.

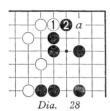
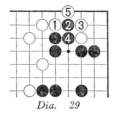
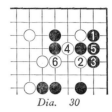

Dia. 28   Dia. 29   Dia. 30

In spite of White 42, my first inclination was not to answer White 44. If I played Black 2 in Dia. 31 and let White defend the center with 3, then later on White *a*, Black *b*, White *c*, Black *d* would be his sente on the upper edge, and he would have made profit in two places. Compare this with Dia. 32, where White defends the center with 1 and lets me play 2. Now Black *a*, White *b*, Black *c*, White *d* would be my sente, and I would be six points better off than in Dia. 31.

This was a close game, and if White was going to take the profit on the upper edge, I did not feel like sitting back and letting him defend the center, too. I wanted to play Black 2 in Dia. 31 at 3 instead. Before making up my mind I performed the calculation on the next two pages, but it only bore out my intuitive feeling that Dia. 31 would be a losing line of play, making my next move inevitable.

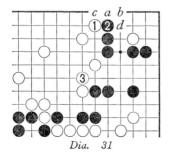
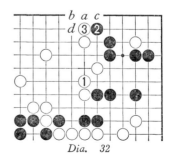

Dia. 31   Dia. 32

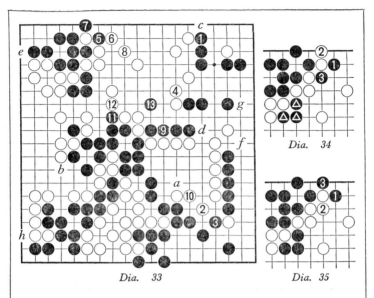

Dia. 33

Dia. 34

Dia. 35

Could I play Black 1 in Dia. 33 and still win? I worked this question out in my head as follows. I imagined White making a forcing move at 2, then taking the big point in the center at 4. Next I could capture with 5 and 7 in sente, since if White omitted 8, I could clamp him with 1 in Dia. 34. He could not cut me off with 2 because the stones marked ⬤ would make the cut at 3 work. He would have to connect at 2 in Dia. 35 and let me link up at 3, but then he would lose a lot of territory. The clamping move at 1 is a useful endgame tesuji to remember.

After White 8 in Dia. 33 I could either play 9 and have White live and make some territory with 10, or play 10 myself and have White play 9. The former choice looks better, since Black 9 would enable me to reduce the center with 11 and 13. If White tries to push through and cut Black 13 off, his own stones get captured.

It is not hard to visualize the rest of the endgame from here. After White responded to Black 13, I could reduce his lower right center territory in sente with *a*, and then I would have a choice of several gote plays, of which *b* looks like the biggest. White could play *c*, *d*, *e*, and *f* in sente, and then take gote at *g*. (If I tried to capture White *g*, I would lose my center stones.) The last large point, at *h*, would fall to me. In detail, this works out to the sequence from White 14 to Black 45 in Dia. 36. I completed the boundaries in my mind's eye by putting in the exchanges marked ⚪ and ⚫.

Taking into consideration the stones captured at the points marked ✕, I counted the territories as shown in the table, and I came out five points behind. For practice, you might like to try verifying my counting. Of course this whole sequence was only my first opinion of how the game would go, so the end result I arrived at might be off by a little, but not by as much as five points. That meant that, as I had suspected, Black 1 in Dia. 33 would be a losing move.

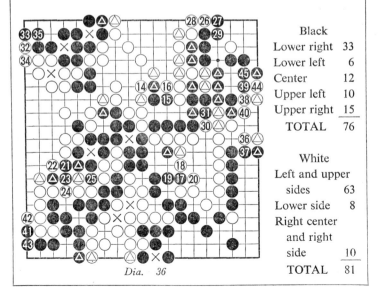

Dia. 36

Black	
Lower right	33
Lower left	6
Center	12
Upper left	10
Upper right	15
TOTAL	76

White	
Left and upper sides	63
Lower side	8
Right center and right side	10
TOTAL	81

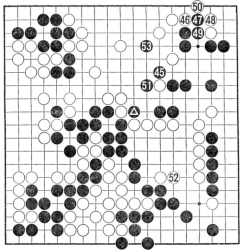

Figure 11 (*145—153*)

I played Black 45. White 46 to 50 hurt, but Black 51 was my sente, picking up the cutting stone ⬣ and forcing White to live with 52. From 45 and 51 I was able to jump out to 53. How would you have answered Black 53?

I suspect that many amateurs would automatically play White 1 in Dia. 37, letting Black make a large-scale capture of White ⬡ with 2 and 4. Look ahead to Figure 12 and see how White resisted with 54. I played Black 55 to keep the option of cutting off the white stone with *a*, but of course Black *a* in Figure 12 would not be as nice as Black 4 in Dia. 37.

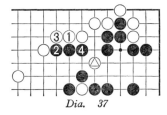

Dia. 37

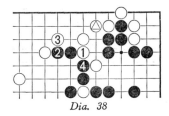

Dia. 38

White did not have to fear Black 2 in Dia. 38. In fact, because of White ○, after 3 and 4 he could take sente and play elsewhere.

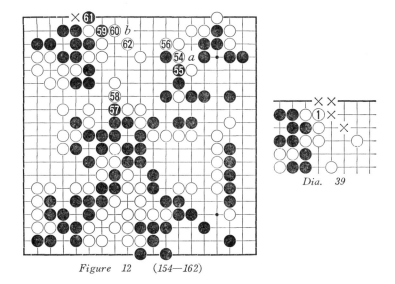

Figure   12   *(154—162)*

When White answered Black 55 at 56, I pushed out at 57 in the center, then took my sente plays at 59 and 61. (White 62 was necessary to prevent Black *b*—see Dia. 34 on page 26.) How much did I gain by this one-stone capture? It enlarged my corner by three points, (two for the prisoner plus one at ×), and reduced White's territory by four points, as you can see by comparing the figure with Dia. 39. That makes only seven points, but I got them in sente, and as a rule of thumb we count double value—fourteen points—for anything gained in sente.

I hope you appreciate the timing of these two moves. If I played them too early, they might not be sente; White might be willing to tolerate being clamped at *b*. If I waited any longer, however, White would connect at 1 in Dia. 39 and I would lose my chance.

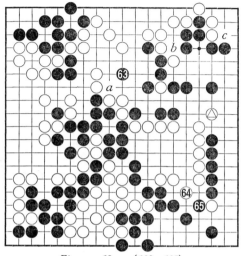

Figure 13 (*163—165*)

My sente profit taken, I went back on the march in the center with Black 63, which threatened to cut at *a*. Now I was putting pressure on White's weaknesses. He played a forcing move at 64, which helped the eye shape of his group in the lower right, and settled down to think.

This was a difficult point in a close game. He had three main plays to consider: he could defend against Black *a*; he could connect at *b*; or he could play *c* in the corner. I counted *b* as being worth a good eight points and *a* and *c* as worth over ten points each, but the exact values were elusive, and I dare say that Kamimura had a hard time making up his mind.

While I was waiting for him to play, I had a look at the right side around White ⬡, but I decided that I had no very big move there. If I tried to enlarge my territory below ⬡ I would only hurt my territory above ⬡, and vice versa.

Let's try to evaluate the three moves that White was considering for his next play. Again, they were (1) to play *c*, (2) to connect at *b*, and (3) to defend against Black *a*.

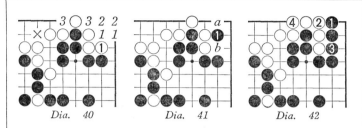

Dia. 40	Dia. 41	Dia. 42

(1) White 1 in Dia. 40. First of all, this adds six or seven points to White's territory: three pairs and possibly the point marked ×. In addition, it weakens Black's corner.

If Black plays here, his best move is 1 in Dia. 41. Whether White should ignore Black 1, answer it at *a*, or answer it at *b* is a hard problem, but let's assume that he ignores it and that Dia. 42 follows in Black's sente. This adds at least four points to Black's territory, as compared with Dia. 40, and strengthens his corner.

White 1 in Dia. 40 is thus worth at least 6+4=10 points in gote, and almost certainly more.

(2) White 1 in Dia. 43. After connecting here, White can push out in sente with *a*, Black *b*, White *c*, Black *d*. Accordingly, if Black plays 1 in Dia. 44, she has gained eight points: the prisoner and the three pairs indicated. She may well have gained more than that, too, since in Dia. 43 White *b* or *d*, instead of *a*, is highly probable.

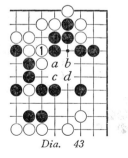

Dia. 43

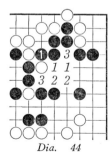

Dia. 44

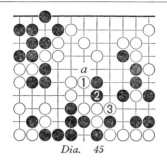

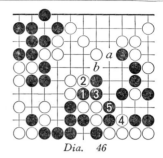

Dia. 45   Dia. 46

(3) White 1 in Dia. 45. This is the hardest of the three plays to figure out. Black would answer it at 2, and White would answer that at 3. How much territory White gains this way is hard to say—Black can still hane at *a*—but at least he has saved three stones from being captured.

If Black plays 1 in Dia. 46, White can answer with 2 and 4. Again an exact calculation is difficult, but if we think of *a* and *b* as Black's sente, then besides the three prisoners, she has taken five more points of territory. In addition, she has linked her groups together, which strengthens her overall board position. The total value of all this must exceed ten points.

The complexities mount when we try to evaluate different combinations of these three plays. Suppose White starts with 1 in Dia. 47, for example. After 2 and 3, Black will play 4 and White

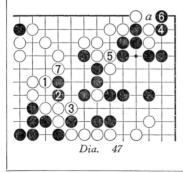

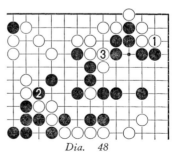

Dia. 47   Dia. 48

will connect at 5. If Black descends to 6, White 7 looks bigger than White *a*.

How does that compare with the simpler sequence shown in Dia. 48? In both diagrams White has gotten two of the original three large plays. In Dia. 47 he has made sizable gains in the center, but at a heavy cost in the corner. For a precise comparison it would be necessary to read out the plays that would follow each diagram, taking the whole board into account, an exercise which we shall forgo.

It is worth taking a closer look at the middle right side, not to see how big it was, but to see how small it was. Suppose Black went first. The exchange of 1 for 2 in Dia. 49 would enlarge her upper territory, but undermine her lower one, since from 2 White could slide in to *a*. Likewise, the exchange in Dia. 50 would undermine her upper territory. If she plays here at all, then 1, 3, and 5 in Dia. 51 would be better, but most of what they gain disappears when White hanes at 6. If the three plays considered in the box above were in the ten-point class, then a black, and therefore a white, play here would be only in the five-point class.

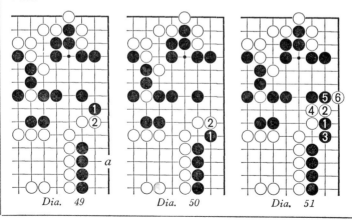

Dia. 49   Dia. 50   Dia. 51

— 33 —

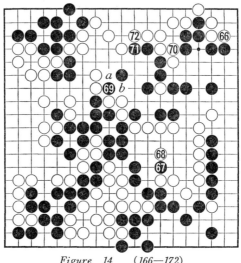

Figure 14 *(166—172)*

Before playing White 66, Kamimura must have tested out many different sequences, and he probably tried to work out what the rest of the endgame would come to after each one, to see whether it would leave him ahead, or at least in contention. Professionals do that constantly. There was more to this position than I could possibly explain, but one thing to note is that in the sequence Kamimura chose, White 66 and 70 reinforced each other, combining to promise further depredations against what was left of my corner.

Before cutting at 69, I made a forcing move at Black 67, and I would like you to remember White's answer at 68. Would you have played there, or would White 1 in Dia. 52 on the next page have come naturally to you? White's territory is about two points smaller in Dia. 52 than in Dia. 53, and if Black plays 2 at 3 in Dia. 53, White can simply cut her off by wedging in at 2. If you don't already know it, learn the clamping move at White 1 in Dia. 53. It is a frequently used endgame tesuji in the center.

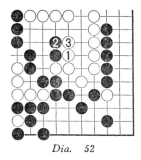

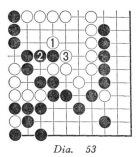

Dia. 52   Dia. 53

Returning to the figure, notice that White did not give atari at *a* and force me to connect at *b*. The reason was that he was saving himself the other atari, at *b*; it is standard practice in a position like this to leave both options open. White *b* would not accomplish anything in the figure, but suppose I had gone on after White 72 to play Black 1 in Dia. 54. Then White 2 and 4 would have made a beautiful combination.

I needed to add one more stone to put my newly-won center territory in order, but as long as White was keeping *a* and *b* open, my hands seemed to be tied. Finally, however, I found a move that would force White to exchange *a* for *b* and enable me not only to complete my own center territory, but to reduce his a little as well. Would you like to try to guess what it was before turning the page?

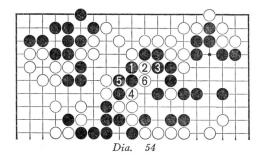

Dia. 54

— 35 —

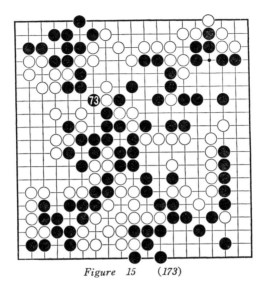

Figure   15   (173)

I played the hane at 73.   After White had taken the two big points in the upper right corner, this was a saving move for me.

White could not cut me off with 1 in Dia. 55 because of the nose tesuji at 2.   If he tried to go to the right with 3, he would suffer a real tragedy, and if he tried to go to the left with 3 in Dia. 56, I would link up with 4 to 10.

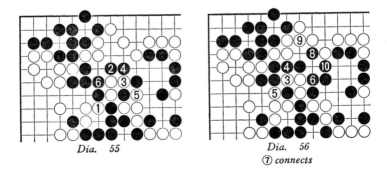

Dia.   55

Dia.   56
⑦ *connects*

— 36 —

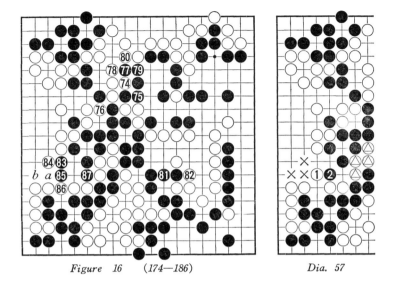

Figure 16   (174—186)   Dia. 57

First White had to give atari at 74, and then he could cut at 76. I came back with Black 77, however, and he could not cut me off at 79, but had to give way with 78. I made a nice profit out of these plays, thanks to my sacrifice at 73.

I followed them up with Black 83 to 87, which reduced White's territory by three points (assume Black *a*, White *b*) as compared with White's playing 1 in Dia. 57. Three points may seem small, but in the first place, White 1 in Dia. 57 would have been sente; I would have had to answer at 2 to keep the four stones marked ◎ captured. Black 83 to 87 were what are called reverse sente plays; they were gote, but they stopped a sente play by the enemy. Just as sente plays have double value, so do reverse sente ones, so the three points here were equivalent to six points in pure gote.

In the second place, Black 83 to 87 created weaknesses in White's position that were to have repercussions all the way over on the upper edge, as we shall shortly see.

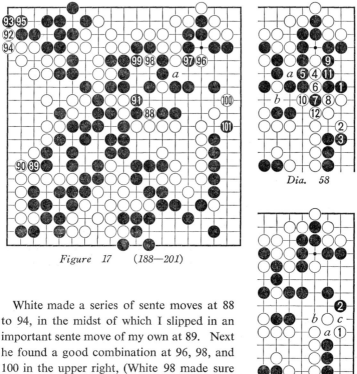

Figure 17   *(188—201)*

White made a series of sente moves at 88 to 94, in the midst of which I slipped in an important sente move of my own at 89. Next he found a good combination at 96, 98, and 100 in the upper right, (White 98 made sure that White *a* would be sente), and now I abandoned what little I had left there and played 101.

Even if I had defended at 1 in Dia. 58, I could only have saved about four points of territory. After forcing me with 2, White would crawl forward to 4, and with *a* his sente, I would have to play 5 and let him escape with 6. Considering the prisoner taken at 7, the loss suffered at 2, and the fact that White could next pull out his stone at *b*, I would not have made any profit.

On the other hand, if White had started with 1 in Dia. 59, I would have answered at 2, threatening Black *a*, which in turn would threaten Black *b* and *c*.

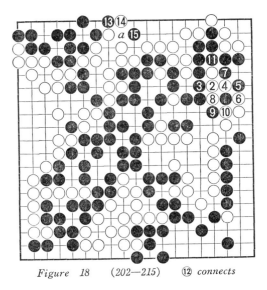

Figure 18   *(202—215)*   ⑫ *connects*

White 2, 4, etc. in Figure 18 destroyed all my territory in the upper right, even taking a prisoner. This was a considerable setback, but then came Black 13 and 15 and my revenge. These two moves were what I had been aiming at when I played Black 83 in Figure 16. White could not connect at *a* without running the risk of the huge ko shown in Dia. 60. Once he got into this ko he would have to ignore any ko threat I made, and I had one or two good ones. I suspect that Kamimura overlooked this sequence, with its squeezing combination at 10 and 12 and throw-in at 14, or he might have played differently earlier.

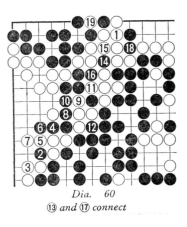

Dia.   60
⑬ *and* ⑰ *connect*

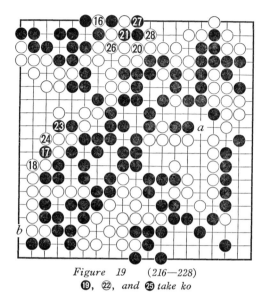

Figure 19   (216—228)

⑲, **㉒**, *and* **㉕** *take ko*

White played 16 and 22 to make me use up two ko threats, but he had to give way and connect at 20 and 26, letting me capture at 27. At the end of this figure it was my turn to play, and there were three large points on the board, at 16, *a*, and *b*. The analysis is complicated, but *a* was the largest, 16 the second largest, and *b* the smallest.

The first step in analyzing the three plays is to examine each individually, as follows.

(1) Black 1 in Dia. 61 is worth six points in gote. Compare Dia. 62, where White 1 captures three black stones.

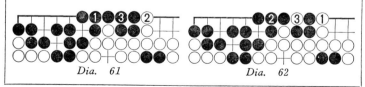

Dia.   61   *Dia.   62*

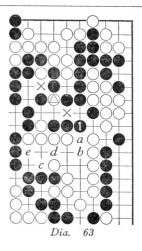

Dia. 63

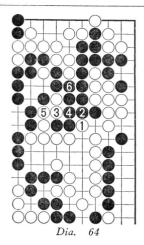

Dia. 64

(2) Black 1 in Dia. 63 is worth four points in reverse sente, or up to 9½ points in gote. For comparison, first I assume that White plays 1 in Dia. 64 and I answer at 2. White 3 and 5 destroy four points of my territory in sente: the two points marked × and the prisoner marked ⊘ in Dia. 63.

Next I try ignoring White 1, as in Dia. 65. White carries on with 3, 5, and 7. Again my territory is four points smaller, and now White's is five points larger than in Dia. 63. In Dia. 65 I will later exchange *a* for *b*. In Dia. 63 I can play *a*, White *b*, Black *c*, White *d*. That leaves me a possible point at *e*, which I count as half a point since I may or may not get it. The total difference between Dias. 63 and 65 is therefore $4+5+\frac{1}{2}=9\frac{1}{2}$ points.

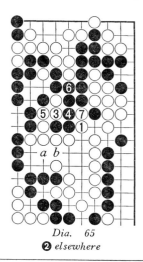

Dia. 65
❷ *elsewhere*

— 41 —

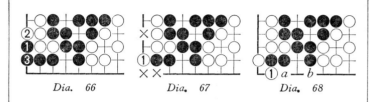

Dia. 66   Dia. 67   Dia. 68

(3)   Black 1 in Dia. 66 is worth three points in reverse sente. If White played 1 in Dia. 67, he would immediately enlarge his territory by the point marked × on the left edge and reduce my territory by the two points marked × on the lower edge.   Furthermore, if I did not answer White 1 in Dia. 67, he could continue with 1 in Dia. 68.   In Dia. 68, if I gave atari at *a*, then White *b* would threaten a snap-back, while if I played *b*, then White *a* would be an atari, and either way I would end up with almost nothing on the lower edge.

Now that we have seen what these three plays have to offer individually, we can put together such possible combinations as the following, (the lettering comes from Dia. 69 on the next page):

I.   I take *A*; White takes *B*; I take *C*, ending in gote.   This is the simplest sequence, and we shall use it as a point of reference.

II.   I take *D* (plus 6); White takes *A*, I answer at *E*, and White plays *F* in sente (minus 4) then *G* (minus 3).   I end in gote because I still have to defend the lower edge against White 1 in Dia. 68, (although first I will play *H* and capture White *A* in sente).   Compared with sequence I, I have come out plus 6 on the upper edge, but minus 7 elsewhere, or one point worse off overall.

III.   I take *D* (plus 6); White takes *A*; I take *C*; White takes *F* then *E* (minus 9½).   This time I come out 3½ points worse off than in sequence I.   I end in sente, but there is nothing left for me to take to get those 3½ points back.

Perhaps any of these sequences would have been good enough to win, but the first sequence was the best.   This was the last hard problem of the endgame.

— 42 —

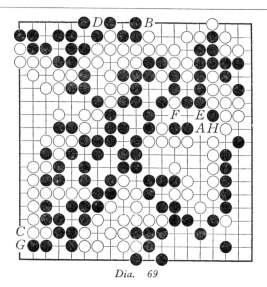

Dia. 69

You may be wondering what the significance of the ko in the last figure was if I was going to let White play *B* in Dia. 69 and capture my three stones. That makes an interesting study. If I had simply played 1 and 3 in Dia. 70, then White would have gotten six points, (three pairs), in an area where he gets only five after playing *B* in Dia. 69, (three black prisoners minus one point for the white stone lost between *B* and *D*). More important, he would have *had* those six points and not needed another move to get them back. If I had played as in Dia. 70 and then taken *A* in Dia. 69, White would have replied at *G* without needing to play *B*, and I might have lost the game.

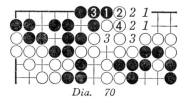

Dia. 70

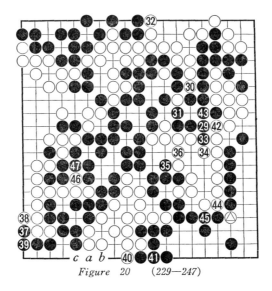

Figure 20   (229—247)

Black 29 to 37 in Figure 20 went according to plan, and the game was now essentially over.   White took sente plays at 40, 42, and 46, each of which reduced my territory, or enlarged his territory, by one point. White 44 gave him some potential ko threats in connection with the stone marked ⚪, and if I had not answered at 45, a white atari at 45 would have reduced my territory by one point in sente.   There was a two-point gote play at *a* for me on the lower edge, but one point in sente is worth two points in gote, and that is why I answered at 45.

Thus White got to play 50 in Figure 21, enlarging his territory by one point and reducing mine by one point as compared with Black *a*, White *b*, and Black *c* in Figure 20.   After this two-point play all the rest of the moves in Figure 21 were worth only one point.   I captured White 48 with 57, but White won it back in the ko there, the moves of which, if we actually played them out, are not recorded.

Now let's calculate the final score.   At the beginning of the endgame I counted my lower right corner as 33 points.   If you remember the boundaries I assumed then, you will see that it had grown by the one point at the right of Black 61, so it was now 34 points.   I had 5 points

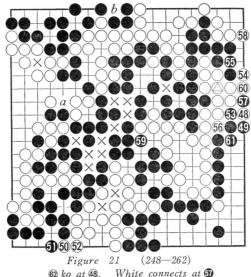

Figure 21 *(248—262)*

⑫ *ko at* ㊽. *White connects at* ㊼

Black		White	
Lower right	34	Left and	
Lower left	5	upper sides	
Upper left	10	Lower side	
Center		Right center	
TOTAL		TOTAL	

in the lower left corner and 10 points in the upper left—precisely my previous estimates. I had acquired a lot of new territory in the center, however; for practice, why don't you see if you can count it yourself? Figure two points, or one pair, for every point where a prisoner has been captured—these points have been marked with ×'s—and one for every other point, including the point under Black 59. Next see if you can count White's territories, noting that he will have to connect at *a*, and remembering to deduct one point for the prisoner he lost at *b* and add one point for the prisoner he captured at △. The three black and three white stones taken in the kos cancel out.

— 45 —

The correct figures are:

Black		White	
Lower right	34	Left and upper	
Lower left	5	sides	58
Upper left	10	Lower side	8
Center	27	Right center	6
TOTAL	76	TOTAL	72

I had won by four points. Reviewing what had happened, I think I came out of the middle game with a lead, but then I made that questionable two-point jump in the left center, (Black 15 in Figure 7) that White was able to cut through, and the game became very close. Both sides played aggressively in the upper right quarter of the board, which led to White's taking territory in what had been my corner and my taking territory in what had been his center. After this exchange, I found the hane at 73 in Figure 15, which gave me a tidy profit, and although later on White came up with a sequence that destroyed all my remaining territory in the upper right corner, I came up with an equally good ko sequence on the upper edge. Perhaps White's failure to notice this last is what let me win.

I have tried to show you the approach that professionals take to the endgame and to give you a taste of the difficulties it involves. Perhaps I have overdone it; I am afraid that you may be feeling a little dismayed right now by all the sequences and calculations. On the other hand, perhaps you have noticed a few things that I had to gloss over. At any rate, before leaving this game behind, I would like to summarize what I think are the main points to be drawn from it.

First of all, you have to appraise the size of individual moves in the endgame. That means reading and counting, as was done several times in the boxes on the previous pages, and it is not always easy. One important principle involved is to take into consideration not only the move itself, but also the subsequent moves that it enables you to play. Another important principle is that a sente, or reverse sente, play has twice the value of a gote play.

Secondly, besides thinking about different moves in isolation, you have to think about them in combination. Ideally you should test out different sequences and calculate to see which gives you the most profit, but even without going to those lengths, you can get in the habit of thinking not in terms like, 'Gee, this is big—I'd better play here,' but in terms like, 'If I play this way I can get two of the three big points, but if I play that way I'll get only one of them,' or like, 'A moment ago there were two big places to play; my opponent has just taken one of them, so instead of answering his move, I'd better take the other,' or like, 'Move A may be much smaller than move B, but it gives me a possible next move which is just as big as B.'

Thirdly, you have to search out your opponent's weaknesses and put pressure on them; that is how you can get profit in sente. Recall White 12, 16, 20–24, 38, 40 etc. and Black 41, 45, 51, 63, etc. in Figures 5 to 13, and you will see that this is what both sides were doing almost constantly. If you cannot find any weaknesses in your opponent's position, try to create some, as White did by probing at 42 (Figure 10) in my upper right corner and as I did by playing 83 (Figure 16) on the left side.

Fourthly, you have to learn to recognize areas that look big, but are largely worthless. One such area in this game was on the right edge, where if I played from one direction, I would only be hurting myself in the other direction, (Dias. 49 and 50).

Fifthly, it helps a great deal to know whether you are ahead or behind. If you know where you stand in the game, you will know whether you can afford to relax, or whether you must put forth some extra effort, or even take risks. If I had gone through this endgame on the assumption that my middle-game lead was holding up, I might never have bothered to hunt for the plays that eventually enabled me to win.

To find out how you stand, you have to count or estimate the territories on the board. I have shown you how I count by pairs, and I recommend this method, although some professionals count directly by two's instead of counting by pairs and doubling the result, and some others count by units of four. Territories that are only vaguely defined can be estimated in multiples of five, which makes adding them up easy. The important thing is to count the territories individually and remember them, instead of trying to count all your territory together and then having to recount everything whenever one territory changes in size.

Sixthly, especially when the game is close or you are behind, you must not accept the ordinary move too readily, but look for the move that gives you a little bit more. Black 173 (Figure 15) and Black 215 (Figure 18) were two places where I did that. Finding such tesujis is, above all, what makes the endgame interesting.

In the next chapter we shall take up counting and calculation again, which cover the first two of these six points. In the third chapter, we shall cover the last point by surveying endgame tesuji. In the final two chapters we shall look at some more games, and give you a chance to try yourself out on them by presenting them as whole-board problems.

CHAPTER 2

Counting

Frequently during the endgame you are faced with a choice of two or three or four moves and must count to find which is the biggest. That sounds simple, but you know by now that it is not—that there can be all sorts of follow-up moves, combinations, and other complications involved. Most important is the question of sente and gote; it is often correct to make a small sente play before a larger gote one. On the basis of sente and gote relationships it is possible to classify moves into four types—gote, sente, reverse sente, and double sente—and we shall begin this chapter by examining each type from a theoretical point of view. Then you will have a chance to apply the theory to some problems.

1. Gote

Gote means gote for both sides, so we are dealing here with situations in which neither player could play in sente. Dia. 1 shows an example from the game in chapter one. As you will recall, a move by one side or the other on the lower edge is worth two points.

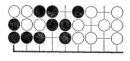

Dia. 1

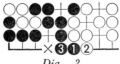

Dia. 2

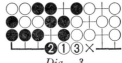

Dia. 3

If Black goes first, he will hane at 1 in Dia. 2, and after White's answer at 2, he will have to connect at 3, ending in gote. If he does not connect at 3, there is no point in his playing 1; he would be better off not playing it at all than playing it and letting White capture it.

If White goes first he will do the same thing, as in Dia. 3. Comparing Dias. 2 and 3, we see that White's territory is one point (marked ×) bigger in Dia. 3 than it was in Dia. 2, and Black's territory is one point (×) bigger in Dia. 2 than in Dia. 3, so the total difference is $1+1=2$ points.

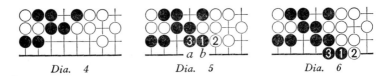

Dia. 4   Dia. 5   Dia. 6

Dia. 4 shows another gote situation—do you know how much this one is worth? The side that plays first here will make a hane on the second line, as Black does in Dia. 5. White answers at 2 and Black connects. In general the solid connection at 3 is better than an open connection at *a* or *b*, because it gives Black essentially the same amount of profit and does not leave White any ko threats.

Dia. 5 does not completely finish the situation. It ends it for the time being, but later on either Black will return to play 1 in Dia. 6 or White will return to play 1 in Dia. 7.

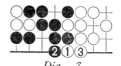

Dia. 7

Dia. 8

Dia. 9

In evaluating Dia. 5, how do we cope with these two possibilities? It would be unfair to White to assume Dia. 6; Black plays two stones in Dia. 6 to White's one, so assuming it would be akin to giving Black an extra move. On the other hand, it would be unfair to Black to assume Dia. 7.

What we do is to strike the mean and assume Black ● and White ○ in Dia. 8. That gives a value exactly halfway between Dias. 6 and 7, and since both sides have been assumed one added stone, neither can complain.

If White goes first, he will play 1 and 3 in Dia. 9, and again we assume ● and ○. The difference between Dias. 8 and 9 is six points: three points of black territory and three points of white. White 1 in Dia. 9, or Black 1 in Dia. 5, is thus worth six points in gote.

What we did in Dia. 8 was to take the mathematical average of Dias. 6 and 7, a procedure that is often needed to get a fair numerical value for a move. We will have to use it, for example, in finding the value of a white connection or black capture at a in Dia. 10. How much do you think this will be worth?

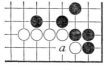

Dia. 10

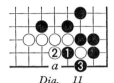

Dia. 11

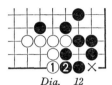

Dia. 12

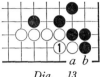

Dia. 13

First let's suppose that Black captures at 1 in Dia. 11. After Black 3, a black hane at *a* would be gote, so it is fair to assume that White 1 and Black 2 in Dia. 12 will finish off the lower edge. In fact, at the proper time, White's descent to 1 should be sente, since it threatens an atari at 2.

Next let's suppose that White connects at 1 in Dia. 13. This is where the averaging comes in, because there is a fairly large hane left for someone in Black *a* or White *b*. There is no special reason to assume that either side will get to make it, so we have to take the average. The easiest way to do this in practice is the following.

First assume that Black answers White's connection, by playing 2 in Dia. 14, and count to see how much White has gained. Black's territory is three points larger in Dia. 12—a pair for the prisoner plus the point marked ×—than in Dia. 14, and White's is one line (two points) smaller. That makes five points, and tells us that in the unlikely event that Black really does answer White 1 in Dia. 14 immediately, White has gained five points in sente.

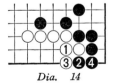

Dia. 14

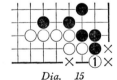

Dia. 15

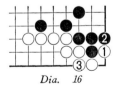

Dia. 16

Next determine the value of White's second move, the hane at 1 in Dia. 15. This is also a move that we met in chapter one, and you may remember the value three points; it enlarges White's territory by one point and reduces Black's territory by two points, all marked ×, in comparison with Dia. 14. White 1 is worth a little more than that, however, because White may be able to make the further hane at 1 in Dia. 16 and reduce Black's territory by one more point. Of course he has to win a ko to keep this extra point, and White 1 in Dia. 16 is gote to begin with, so we cannot add on too much for it, but at least we can count White 1 in Dia. 15 as being worth 3 (+) points in gote.

Finally, to take the average of Dias. 14 and 15, add half the value of White 1 in Dia. 15 to the figure obtained in Dia. 14. Half of 3 (+) is $1\frac{1}{2}(+)$, or 2 (−), so the sum is

$$5+2(-)=7(-).$$

That is the value of White 1 in Dia. 13 or Black 1 in Dia. 11.

During actual play you are not going to have to go through a lot of computations like the above before you put down every stone, thank goodness, but there are times when it would be very helpful to know the value of a move like 1 in Dia. 11 or 13. With a little practice, you should be able to make the necessary calculations quickly and easily, and even if you get a slightly wrong answer, going through the process will have forced you to think about the moves in a logical way, and that in itself will be valuable. You will learn shortcuts, too, such as 'White 1 in Dia. 13 is essentially like the hane and connection in Dias. 4 to 9, which was worth six points, except that the hane in Dia. 15 is a point or two bigger than an ordinary hane on the first line, so I'll add on one extra and call it seven.'

When the following move is made in sente instead of gote, you count in its full value instead of only half. You should understand that fact from the previous chapter. In light of it, let's take another look at a hane and connection on the second line.

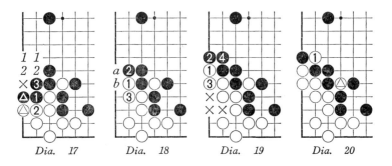

Dia. 17   Dia. 18   Dia. 19   Dia. 20

What is the value of Black 1 and 3 in Dia. 17? If Black plays these two moves, we can make the standard assumption of Black ⊕ and White ⊘ to finish off the edge. If White plays 1 and 3 in Dia. 18, however, we cannot assume Black *a* and White *b*, because now White can play *a* in sente.

The correct assumption is White 1 to Black 4 in Dia. 19. (If Black does not connect at 4, White will cut at 1 in Dia. 20, and because of the stone marked ⊘, Black will be in a lot of trouble). Since Black and White have played two stones apiece in Dia. 19, this is fair.

Comparing Dias. 17 and 19, you can see that Dia. 17 makes Black's territory five points larger, (two pairs plus the point marked ×), and White's three points smaller. Black 1 in Dia. 17 is thus worth eight points In general, the value of a hane and connection on the second line varies from six points on up, depending on what the follow-up moves are and whether they are sente or not.

For future reference, notice that in a gote situation, there is a difference of two stones between one side's playing first and the other side's playing first. In Dia. 17, for instance, Black has played two stones and White one, while in Dia. 18 Black has played one stone and White two.

2. Sente

In this section we shall be dealing with one-sided sente situations, where one side has a sente move, but the other side has only a gote move. Dia. 1 shows one such.

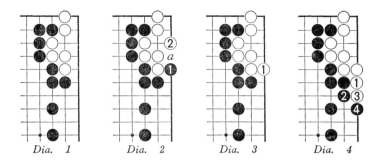

Dia. 1   Dia. 2   Dia. 3   Dia. 4

The side with the sente move here is Black; when he hanes at 1 in Dia. 2, White must answer as shown to save his corner. He cannot play 2 at *a*, or Black will step over him by playing 2 (atari!) and kill him. How much is Black 1, which reduces White's corner territory to three points, worth?

If White gets a chance to play here, his move is the descent to 1 in Dia. 3. Now his corner territory is five points, two points larger than before. White 1 is gote, but White can presumably push out at 1 and 3 in Dia. 4 in sente, so we have to count that in when figuring the value of Dia. 3. Dia. 4 reduces Black's territory by three points, making the total value here 2+3=5 points.

Moreover, the difference in the number of stones played in Dias. 2 and 3 is only one; in both diagrams White has played one stone, while Black has played one stone in Dia. 2 and no stones in Dia. 3. This is why a sente play is considered to have twice the value of a gote play. Black 1 in Dia. 2, (five points in sente), would be worth more, for example, than Black 1 in Dia. 17 on the previous page, (eight points in gote). We can even put this in mathematical terms:

$$\frac{5 \text{ points}}{1 \text{ stone}} > \frac{8 \text{ points}}{2 \text{ stones}}$$

The problem with a sente move is not so much its exact value as the proper time to play it: too early, and it may not be answered; too late, and the chance may be lost. You will recall several examples from chapter one, including the position shown in Dia. 5. White had two sente moves there: a small one at *a* and a large one at *b*. He played the latter—White 1 in Dia. 6—as soon as he could, and Black had to answer it because it threatened to kill the corner. He saved the former—White 1 in Dia. 7—for much later, because it was relatively small and because the threat that it involved was only to destroy about four points of Black's territory, not enough to make it sente if played too early.

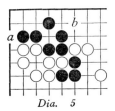

Dia. 5

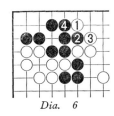

Dia. 6

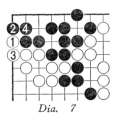

Dia. 7

Taking into consideration the size of the move itself and the size of the threat behind it, we can identify four cases:

1. Big move, big threat (Dia. 6, for example). Play these early—they are important.

2. Big move, moderate threat. Play these as early as the bigness of the move warrants, but don't count on your opponent answering the threat.

3. Small move, big threat (Dia. 2, for example). Here you have a lot of leeway; you can play the move early and your opponent will answer the big threat, or you can leave it for later and he will not give up his turn to take the small move away from you. You should leave such moves unplayed for a while at least—they make good ko threats—but remember that they are worth as much as gote moves twice their size, and don't leave them so long that your opponent plays them instead of you.

4. Small move, small threat (Dia. 7, for example). Save these, of course, until the appropriate time.

Occasionally you will make what you expect to be a sente play and be surprised to have it ignored. This does not mean that it was a mistake. Your opponent may be going to answer it, but after making some forcing moves of his own first, or he may have decided to try for some kind of exchange. A good player knows that if he answers all his opponent's moves, he will be taking one loss after another right through the whole endgame, so he is constantly on the lookout for chances to ignore them, play elsewhere, and make some profit of his own.

3. Reverse Sente

A reverse sente play is, as the name says, the reverse of a sente play: one made by the gote side in a one-sided sente situation. White 1 in Dia. 1 is worth five points in reverse sente. It is gote, but it stops Black 1 in Dia. 2, which would be sente.

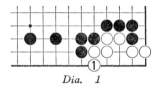

Dia. 1

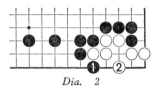

Dia. 2

A reverse sente play has the same double value as a sente play, and for the same reason—that there is a difference of only one stone between it and the enemy's playing in sente. White 1 in Dia. 1 has, in theory, the same value as a ten-point gote play:

$$\frac{5 \text{ points}}{1 \text{ stone}} = \frac{10 \text{ points}}{2 \text{ stones}}$$

This means that, in theory, White should prefer it to any gote play worth less than ten points.

The opportunity to make a reverse sente play usually arises when the enemy's sente move is not backed up by a very big threat. In the game in chapter one, you will remember that Black made the reverse sente play at 1 to 5 in Dia. 3.

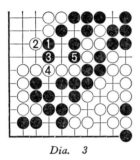

Dia. 3

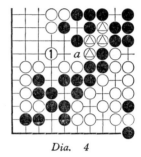

Dia. 4

White would have liked to play 1 in Dia. 4 in sente, but the threat behind it, to connect at *a* and rescue the four stones marked ⬨, was worth only about eight plus one or two, say ten points, which would not have been enough to make Black answer it early in the game. When the endgame reached the ten-point level White was busy in the upper half of the board, and Black emerged from there with sente to play Dia. 3.

Reverse sente opportunities like this are a common occurrence. Even though reverse sente moves are gote, you should not think of them as gote; they really are about twice as valuable as ordinary gote moves, a fact which the problems in the second half of this chapter will support.

4. Double Sente

A double sente situation is one in which either side can play in sente. In Dia. 1 on the next page, for example, White can hane at 1 and connect at 3, and if Black does not answer at 2 and 4, he loses a large amount of territory. Similarly, Black can hane at 1 and connect at 3 in Dia. 2, and if White does not answer at 2 and 4, his corner group is in danger. (If he plays 2 and omits 4, he cannot be killed unconditionally, as Dia. 3 shows, but the ko is still a sizable threat.) Comparing Dias. 1 and 2, we see that the difference is two points of black territory and two points of white territory, or four points in all.

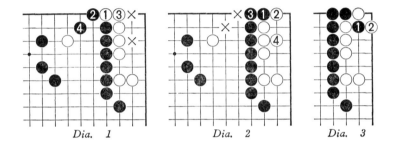

Dia. 1   Dia. 2   Dia. 3

If we compare the number of stones played, however, we find no difference at all. In both diagrams Black and White have played two stones apiece. If we try to divide the number of points gained by the number of stones difference, as we have been doing so far, we get:

$$\frac{4 \text{ points}}{0 \text{ stones}} = \text{infinity (?)}$$

What this means is that whoever makes the hane, White in Dia. 1 or Black in Dia. 2, is getting something for nothing. Double sente moves are the prize points on the board, and both players try to take them as early as possible.

How early can they be taken? That depends, of course, on the size of the threats that follow them. The bigger the threat, the earlier the move can be made in sente.

How early the move should be made is another question. In Dia. 4 we have the same double sente situation at *a-b* on the upper edge, except that now White still has a lot of scope for activity in the stone marked ◎; consider White *c*, for instance. It would be a crime for him to play 1 and 3 in Dia. 5; he would only be hurting his chances to do something bigger in this area. He should abstain, therefore, even if it means enduring Black *b* in Dia. 4.

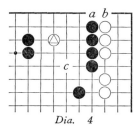

Dia. 4

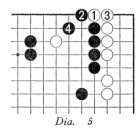

Dia. 5

Still, the competition to take double sente points tends to be rather intense. In the game in chapter one, you will remember, a double sente point arose at *a* in Dia. 6. If White played there he would be threatening to jump into Black's corner, and if Black played there he would be threatening to jump into White's upper side. It was White's turn, and although there was a larger gote move at *b*, he felt he could not put off *a*, so he played it before it was really sente, and the exchange in Dia. 7 followed. Such exchanges are natural in close games.

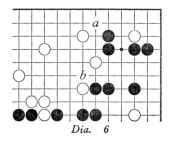

Dia. 6

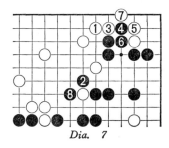

Dia. 7

5. Problems

Now you can apply what you have learned to the following problems. In each one three possible moves are marked *A*, *B*, and *C*; assume that there is nothing else worth considering on the board and try to figure out the best sequence in which to play them.

Your first step should be to examine the moves one by one and determine how much each is worth and whether it is gote, sente, or whatnot. Next you should experiment with different sequences and try to find the one that gives you the most profit. Finally, in order to score yourself, identify the largest move—not necessarily the largest in absolute value, but the one you should play first in the optimal sequence—and the smallest move—the one that comes last of the three in the optimal sequence—and try to assign a numerical value—4 points in double sente, for example—to each move. After turning the page and reading the answer, give yourself ten points if you correctly identified the largest move and ten points if you correctly identified the smallest move, then subtract the total amount by which your numerical values were off the mark. Twenty points is thus the perfect score for each problem, and there is a scoring chart at the end.

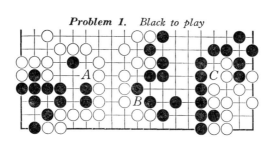

Problem 1. *Black to play*

Largest move _____   smallest move _____

A: ___ pts. in _____ *B:* ___ pts. in _____ *C:* ___ pts. in _____

Largest move: *C*–2 points in sente.

    Dia. 1. If White does not answer at 2, Black 2 kills him.

    Dia. 2. White 1 would enlarge the corner by 2 points.

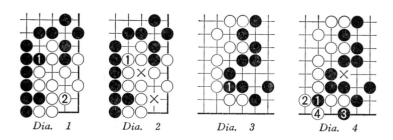

Dia. 1   *Dia. 2*   *Dia. 3*   *Dia. 4*

2nd largest move: *B*–3 points in gote.

    Dia. 3. Although gote, this move has hidden value.

    Dia. 4. Next Black can play 1 and 3 in sente. The reason he cuts at 1, instead of just playing 3 and letting White connect at 1, is to leave a ko threat for himself inside White's territory.

    Dia. 5. White 1 is gote, but it promises 3 in sente. Black's territory is now 1 point smaller than before, and White's territory, assuming ❹ – ⬭, is 2 points larger. An easy way to visualize White's gain is to take Black 1 in Dia. 4 mentally off the board, (one prisoner point), and move White 2 over to occupy its place.

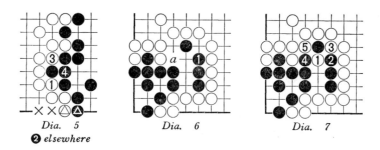

Dia. 5   *Dia. 6*   *Dia. 7*

❷ *elsewhere*

Smallest move: *A*—1½ points in gote.

Dia. 6. Black 1 saves a prisoner, and next Black *a* would make one point of territory.

Dia. 7. White 1 takes a prisoner, but without making any territory.

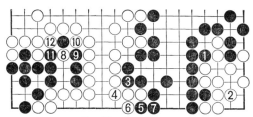

Combination Figure

Combination figure. Black takes his two points in sente at 1, then goes to 3. White's connection at 4 leaves Black 5 and 7, at two points in gote, as the largest plays on the board, so Black makes them and White gets 8. Black has taken *B* and *C*, worth a total of five points. If he had started with *B*, or 3 in the figure, followed by White 1 and Black 9, he would have picked up only four and a half points, which shows how two points in sente can be more valuable than three points in gote.

White 4 at 5 would give the same net result, but from the standpoint of not leaving ko threats, 4 is best.

Problem 2. *White to play*

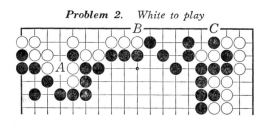

Largest move _____ smallest move _____

A: __ pts. in _____ *B:* __ pts. in _____ *C:* __ pts. in _____

Largest move: *B*—4 points in gote.

Dia. 1. Descending to 1 means that White will not have to connect around *a*, and next he can push out at 3 in sente. Incidentally, if White played 1 at 3, Black could make a throw-in at 1, and then White would have to connect around *a*.

Dia. 2. Black 1 is gote, but 3 and 5 follow automatically. After mentally removing Black 3 and moving White 4 over, we see that White's territory is three points smaller, and Black's one point larger, than in Dia. 1.

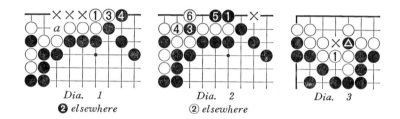

Dia. 1
❷ *elsewhere*

Dia. 2
② *elsewhere*

Dia. 3

2nd largest move: *A*—3 points in gote.

Dia. 3. Connecting at 1 gives White one point of territory at × and two at ⬣, or three in all.

Dia. 4. If Black plays 1 and 3, White immediately loses two of those three points, being left with only the prisoner point at ⬣. White will ignore Black 3, making it gote, but—

Dia. 5. Then Black trades one prisoner for two and takes White's third point away from him.

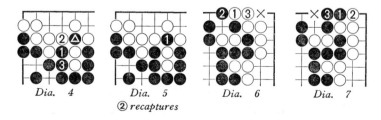

Dia. 4

Dia. 5
② *recaptures*

Dia. 6

Dia. 7

Smallest move: *C*—2 points in gote.

Dia. 6. If Black has his eyes open he will not connect against White 1, but play 2 and make White connect. White has reduced Black's territory by one point in gote.

Dia. 7. Similarly, Black can reduce White's territory by one point in gote. The total value here is two points.

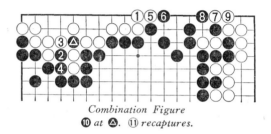

Combination Figure
⑩ *at* ▲. ⑪ *recaptures.*

Combination figure. All three moves are gote, so the players take them in order of absolute value, from largest to smallest. The only possible variation in this sequence is that White could play 7 at 9, threatening 8. Black would defend at 7, and then White could connect at ▲. This would give him one more point in the upper left corner, but one less point in the upper right corner. Either way, White ends the exchange in gote.

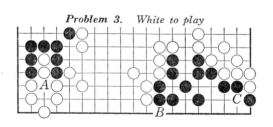

Problem 3. *White to play*

Largest move _____   smallest move _____

A: ___ pts. in _____. *B:* ___ pts. in _____. *C:* ___ pts. in _____.

Largest move: *B*—3 points in reverse sente.

Dia. 1. White 1 makes White's territory two points larger, and Black's territory one point smaller, than if Black got to play here first.

Dia. 2. Thus the value of a move here is three points, but the important thing is that Black can play 1 and 3 in sente. If White omits 4, then Black 4, White *a*, Black *b*, White *c*, and Black can capture White 2 and *a*. That makes White 1 in Dia. 1 a reverse sente play.

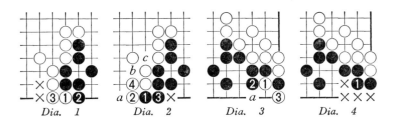

Dia. 1　　Dia. 2　　Dia. 3　　Dia. 4

2nd largest move: *C*—5 (+) points in gote.

Dia. 3. White can reduce Black's territory and take a prisoner, but in gote.

Dia. 4. Black's connection saves him the four points of territory marked ×: add on the prisoner, and the value of Black 1 is five points. This is assuming that Black eventually descends to *a* in Dia. 3.

Dia. 5. Actually, the value is a little more than five. By making the hane at 1 and winning the ko, White may be able to reduce Black's territory by one more point, which adds a 'plus' to the five points counted in Dias. 3–4.

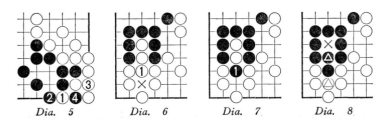

Dia. 5　　Dia. 6　　Dia. 7　　Dia. 8

Smallest move: *A*—4 points in gote.

Dia. 6. By connecting, White keeps the one point of territory marked ×.

Dia. 7. Black 1 takes two prisoners.

Dia. 8. And after connecting at ⬤, Black has one point of territory at ×. He has made one point of territory, destroyed one point of territory, and taken two prisoners for a total gain of four.

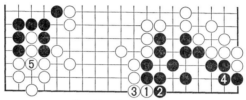

Combination Figure

Combination figure. After White takes the important reverse sente point at 1, he and Black split the two remaining plays, Black taking the larger at 4. The absolute values of White 1 and 5 are three and four respectively, for a total of seven.

If White had started by cutting at 4 and carrying out Dia. 3, Black would have played 3 in sente and captured at 5, getting two of the three plays. White's gain would only be 5 (+) points.

Problem 4. Black to play.

Largest move _____   smallest move _____

A _____   *B* _____   *C* _____

Largest move: *C*—2 (−) points in double sente.

Dia. 1. White will answer Black 1 at 2 to keep Black from continuing at *a* and gaining 4 (+) points in sente.

Dia. 2. Similarly, Black answers White 1 at 2 to stop White *a*. If we assume that White eventually descends to *b*, (and that Black does so in Dia. 1), the difference between Black 1 and White 1 is two points. We have to degrade these two points somewhat for the possibility of Black *b*, but as double sente, they still have top value.

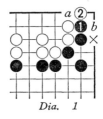

Dia. 1

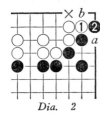

Dia. 2

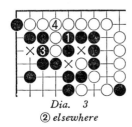

Dia. 3
② *elsewhere*

2nd largest move: *A*—4 points in gote.

Dia. 3. Black 1 is gote, but it makes 3 Black's sente.

Dia. 4. Now 3 is White's sente, White has a point at ×, and Black will eventually have to connect at two additional points around ⬭. That adds up to four points in all.

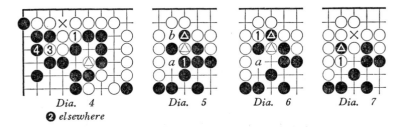

Dia. 4
❷ *elsewhere*

Dia. 5

Dia. 6

Dia. 7

Smallest move: *B*—3½ points in gote.

Dia. 5. Black 1 saves ⬤ and captures ⬭, but does not make any territory because *a* and *b* are miai.

— 68 —

Dia. 6. White 1 saves ◎ and captures ▲, which makes a difference of two points so far, and there is a further play left at *a*.

Dia. 7. That play is worth three points—two at ▲ and one at ×— but it is gote, so only half its value should be added on. White 1 in Dia. 6, or Black 1 in Dia. 5, is worth:

$$2+(\tfrac{1}{2}\times3)=3\tfrac{1}{2} \text{ points in gote.}$$

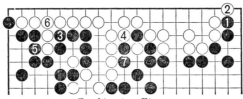

Combination Figure

Combination figure.   Black plays 1 in sente, then 3, and answers 4 at 7, so all White manages to get are the two points noted in Dia. 6. If Black had begun at 3, White would have gotten both 1 and 4, gaining 4(−) points. Worse yet, if Black had begun by playing at the right of 7, White would have gotten 1 and 3, gaining 6(−) points.

Problem 5.   White to play.

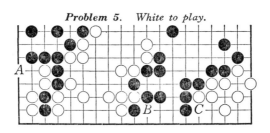

Largest move _____   smallest move _____

A _____   *B* _____   *C* _____

Largest move: *A*—7 points in gote.

Dia. 1. Assume Black *a* and White *b* later.

Dia. 2. Black 1 and 3 are gote, but they leave two white stones in atari. To compute their value, first imagine that White connects at ⊘. Assuming *a-b* at the edge, Black's territory is two points larger than in Dia. 1, and White's is three points smaller, (at *b*, ⊘, and 2). That makes five.

Dia. 3. Next, if Black captures at 1, he gains another four points in gote. Adding in half of this, we get:

$$5+(\tfrac{1}{2}\times4)=7 \text{ points in gote.}$$

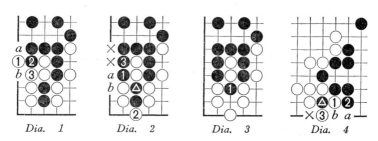

Dia. 1   *Dia. 2*   *Dia. 3*   *Dia. 4*

2nd largest move: *B*—6 points in gote.

Dia. 4. Since White cannot hane at *a* in sente, we can assume Black *a* and White *b*. White has gained three points of territory: two at ⊘ and one at ×.

Dia. 5. By connecting at 1, Black also gains three points of territory, so the total value is six points.

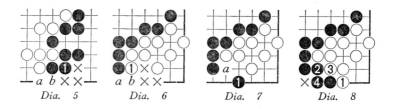

Dia. 5   *Dia. 6*   *Dia. 7*   *Dia. 8*

Smallest move: *C*—4 points in gote.

Dia. 6. After White 1, assume Black *a* and White *b*.

Dia. 7. By playing 1, (or *a*—White ignores either move), Black can destroy the three points marked × in Dia. 6.

Dia. 8. Toward the end of the game the exchange from 1 to 4 is reasonable, so Black has augmented his own territory at ×, bringing the total value of Black 1 in Dia. 7, or White 1 in Dia. 6, to four points.

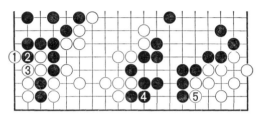

Combination Figure

Combination figure. Having the first move, White gets two of the three large plays. Black's only gain is six points for connecting at 4. If White began at 4, Black would take Dia. 2, gaining five points, and next Dias. 3 and 7 would be miai, so Black would get one of them, bringing his total to nine points.

Problem 6.   *Black to play.*

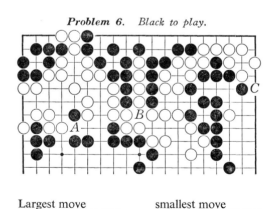

Largest move _____   smallest move _____

A _____   *B* _____   *C* _____

— 71 —

Largest move: *C*—5 points in reverse sente.

Dia. 1. Black 1 saves four points of friendly territory, and later on Black can play *a* in sente to rob White of ×.

Dia. 2. White 1 to 5 are sente. Black cannot afford to answer 1 at 3, because he would be risking considerably more than White in the ensuing ko fight.

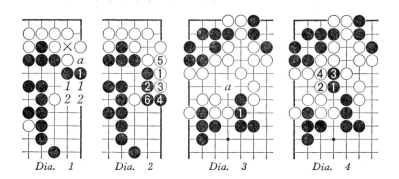

Dia. 1   Dia. 2   Dia. 3   Dia. 4

2nd largest move: *A*—8 points in gote.

Dia. 3. If Black played 1, White would probably not defend at *a*, which would save only three points.

Dia. 4. So Black could keep on in sente as shown.

Dia. 5. Comparing this diagram with the last, we see that White 1 saves eight points: two at ⬤ plus three more pairs.

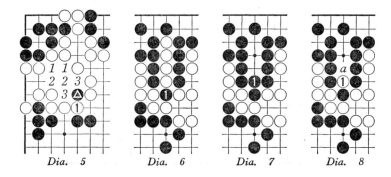

Dia. 5   Dia. 6   Dia. 7   Dia. 8

Smallest move: *B*—6(−) points in gote.

Dia. 6. Black 1 may look bigger than it really is.

Dia. 7. Even if Black connects at 1, he only gains seven points: four prisoners and three points of territory.

Dia. 8. If White recaptures at 1, Black's gain drops to five points, or four if White also gets to play *a*. Both Dias. 7 and 8 are gote, so we average them to obtain 6(−) as the value of Black 1 in Dia. 6.

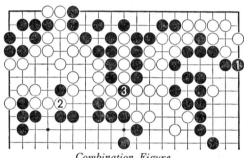

Combination Figure

Combination figure. By starting with the reverse sente play, Black is able to take two of the three large moves for a total gain of about eleven points. If he had started with 2, White would have played 1 in sente, then 3, and Black's gain would have been only eight points.

Problem 7. White to play.

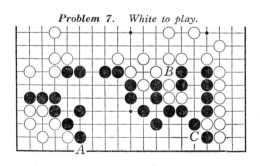

Largest move _____   smallest move _____

A _____   B _____   C _____

Largest move: *A*—4(+) points in double sente.

Dia. 1. White can play 1 and 3 in sente.

Dia. 2. Similarly, Black 1 threatens to kill the corner. The difference between these two diagrams is the four points marked ×, plus a little more since in Dia. 2 White may have to give up another point to avoid a seki.

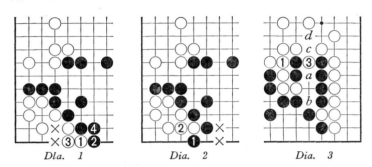

Dia. 1   *Dia. 2*   *Dia. 3*

2nd largest move: *B*—11 points in gote.

Dia. 3. White 1 rescues three white stones, and if Black plays elsewhere White can follow with 3, capturing two black stones. (If Black tries to connect at *a*, White plays *b*.) White 3 is worth six points in gote, as compared with Black 3 followed by Black *c*, White *d*.

Dia. 4. Assuming Black *a*, White *b* in this diagram, the total difference between it and Dia. 3 is fourteen points: nine points of black territory, (three prisoners plus the ×'s), and five points of white territory,

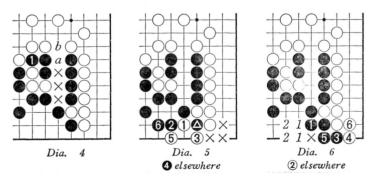

Dia. 4

Dia. 5
❹ *elsewhere*

Dia. 6
② *elsewhere*

— 74 —

(two prisoners plus *c* in Dia. 3), but since White 3 in Dia. 3 is gote, only half its value, three points instead of six, should be counted. White or Black 1 is therefore worth 14−3=11 points in gote.

Smallest move: *C*—10 points in gote.

Dia. 5. White 1 means five points of territory for White: two for capturing ⬣ and three for the ×'s.

Dia. 6. Black 1 likewise means five points, so the value of a move by either side here is ten points.

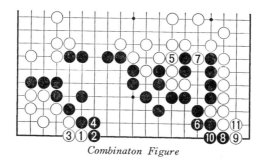

Combinaton Figure

Combination figure. White gains four points at 1 and 3, then fourteen points at 5 and 7, making eighteen in all.

Problem 8. *Black to play*

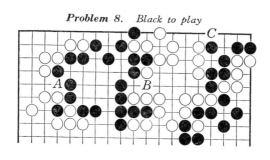

Largest move _____ smallest move _____

A _____ B _____ C _____

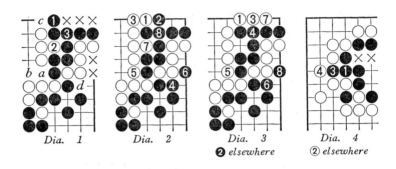

Dia. 1	Dia. 2	Dia. 3	Dia. 4
		❷ elsewhere	**②** elsewhere

Largest move: *C*—6 points in gote.

Dia. 1. Black must answer White 2 at 3, or a white throw-in there is fatal. After this Black *a*, White *b*, and then White *c*, Black *d* are a fair assumption to make.

Dia. 2. Suppose White plays 1. If Black replies at 2, he has to keep on at 4, 6, and 8. White has erased two of the points marked × in Dia. 1 and been able to play both 3 and 5 instead of just one of them, so his total gain is three.

Dia. 3. If Black ignores White 1, White continues with 3, 5, and 7 in sente and Black loses the other three points marked × in Dia. 1, bringing the total difference between Dias. 1 and 3 to six points in gote.

2nd largest move: *A*—5(−) points in gote.

Dia. 4. Black 1 promises Black 3.

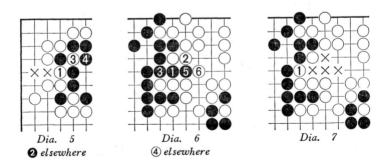

Dia. 5	Dia. 6	Dia. 7
❷ elsewhere	**④** elsewhere	

— 76 —

Dia. 5. White's territory is now two points larger than before, Black's is two points smaller, and White has captured a prisoner, making a total difference of five points. Since Black may be able to recapture the prisoner, we count this as 5(−).

Smallest move: *B*—4 points in gote.

Dia. 6. Black 1 gains nothing without 3, so it is gote.

Dia. 7. White 1, also gote, saves four points.

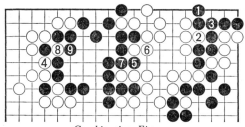

Combination Figure

Combination figure. In the best sequence Black takes the largest and smallest plays. Consider these alternatives:

i)   Black 4, White 1, Black 5 and 7, White plays Dia. 3. Black has gained 5 (−) on the left but lost 6 on the right.

ii)   Black 4, White 1, Black plays Dia. 2, White 7. Black has gained 5 (−) on the left but lost 4+3=7 on the right.

Problem 9. *Black to play.*

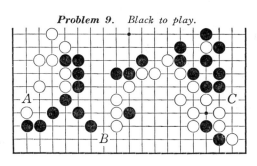

Largest move _____   smallest move _____

A _____   *B* _____   *C* _____

Largest move: *B*—6 points in double sente.

Dia. 1. White cannot afford to ignore Black 1, and Black 3 and 5 are also sente. White *a*, Black *b* will come later.

Dia. 2. White could perform the same maneuver in sente. The difference is three points of territory on each side, or six in all.

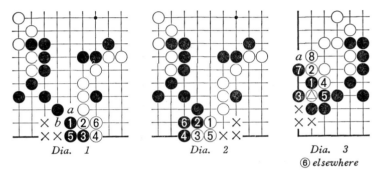

Dia. 1   Dia. 2   Dia. 3

⑥ *elsewhere*

2nd largest move: *A*—10 points in gote.

Dia. 3. Black has gained five points of territory: two for ◯ and three others. Later, *a* will be White's sente.

Dia. 4. White also gains five points of territory if he plays first, so the total value here is ten.

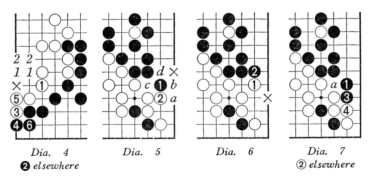

Dia. 4   Dia. 5   Dia. 6   Dia. 7

❷ *elsewhere*   ② *elsewhere*

Smallest move: *C*—2 points in double sente.

Dia. 5. Since Black cannot play *a* in sente, assume White *a*, Black *b*, and, of course, White *c*, Black *d*.

Dia. 6. Making assumptions similar to those in Dia. 5, we find that the difference between Dias. 5 and 6 is only one point of territory on each side, or two in all.

Dia. 7. Black 1 is not necessarily sente, either. If White ignores it, the 3–4 exchange costs him only three additional points, (averaging Black *a* and White *a*). That is, Black 1 and 3 put together gain only 2+3=5 points.

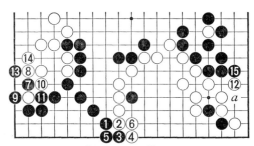

Combination Figure

Combination figure. Black takes both big points with 1 and 7 while White gains only a small amount on the right edge. Some alternatives:

i) Black plays 7 at 12, White 10, Black *a*. Black has given up ten points on the left side to get only five on the right.

ii) Black plays 1 at 7, White plays 1, 8, 10, and 12. By letting White play 1, Black has lost six points.

iii) Black plays 1 at 12, White plays 1 and 10, Black plays *a*. He has given up 6+10=16 points to gain only five.

Scoring Chart

Problem	1	2	3	4	5	6	7	8	9	total
Your score										

Total	50	60	70	80	90	100	110	120	130	140	150	160	170
Rank	8 kyu	7	6	5	4	3	2	1 kyu	1 dan	2	3	4	5 dan

CHAPTER 3

Endgame Tesuji

The endgame has its own special brand of tesuji, mostly concerned with the edge of the board. Many of them are only one or two points better than the more obvious alternative plays, but if you go through the endgame losing one point here, two points there, and so on at every turn, your losses can quickly mount up. On the other hand, if you can outplay your opponent by just a couple of points in half a dozen places, you can overtake a ten-point lead.

Defending Territory

Dia. 1. White has just come sliding into Black's upper right corner with △. Do you know the correct response?

Dia. 2. Your first reaction might be this diagonal play, but White can jump in front of it with 2 and do plenty of damage.

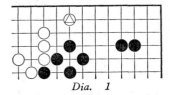

Dia. 1

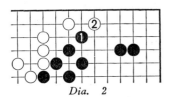

Dia. 2

Dia. 3. (next page) An aggressive player might try this contact play, but it leads to an exchange, White living with 2 to 8. The question is how much Black can do in return to the white territory to the left. Depending on the answer, Black 1 could be the best move, and White might have to draw back to 5 instead of bending out at 2, but the odds are that Black has taken a loss.

Dia. 4. If there were a black stone at *a*, this inside contact play would be a tesuji—White would have to reply at *b* and Black could then play *c*—but as things stand White can play 2 and Black's position has worsened considerably.

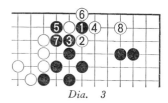

Dia. 3

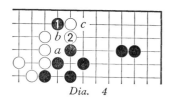

Dia. 4

Dia. 5. The correct move is frequently to confront White on the second line, one space away. White cannot get anywhere with 2, because he runs into the stone marked ▲.

Dia. 6. White 2 here is better, but Black can complete his defense with 3.

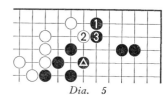

Dia. 5

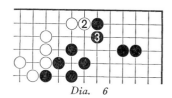

Dia. 6

Problem 1. White to play. How can he defend the largest amount of corner territory?

Problem 2. White could capture two stones by wedging in at the 5–5 point, but he has a better way.

Problem 3. Black to defend the corner.

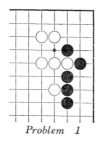

Problem 1

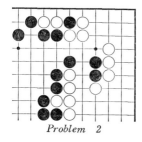

Problem 2

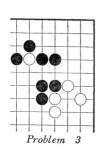

Problem 3

Answer to problem 1. If Black 3, White 2.

Dia. 1a. If White plays 1 here, he lets Black push him around with 2 and 4 and comes out about four points worse off.

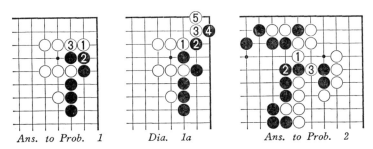

Ans. to Prob. 1   Dia. 1a   Ans. to Prob. 2

Answer to problem 2. The clamp at 1 makes 2 and 3 miai, and no doubt you have already verified that Black 3, White 2, ends badly for Black.

Dia. 2a. Again, the wrong answer is four points worse.

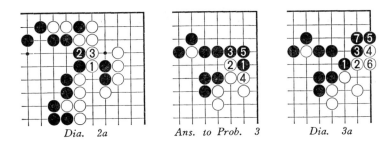

Dia. 2a   Ans. to Prob. 3   Dia. 3a

Answer to problem 3. Black 1 should be the first move that occurs to you in this shape.

Dia. 3a. Black's territory may be the same as before, but White's is two points larger.

Extensions

During the opening, extensions are generally made on the third or fourth line, but during the endgame, they are often made on the second line.

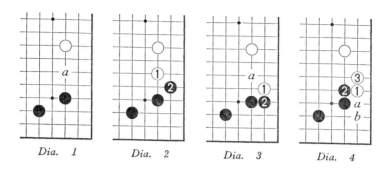

| Dia. 1 | Dia. 2 | Dia. 3 | Dia. 4 |

Dia. 1. During the opening, *a* would be the natural extension point for both sides in this position.

Dia. 2. If White extended to 1 during the endgame, however, Black could reply immediately at 2, and on the edge, at least, White would have gained no profit.

Dia. 3. In the endgame, the correct extension is likely to be the large knight's move on the second line to 1. If Black replies at 2, White can defend at *a* for a large profit, or he can leave this as a forcing exchange and turn elsewhere.

Dia. 4. If Black presses at 2 he can make White reply at 3, but this leaves his corner open to White *a*, *b*, etc.

Problem 1. Black to play. What should he do on the lower edge?

Problem 2. White to play? How should he extend toward Black's very strong corner position?

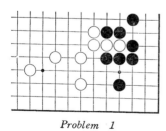

Problem 1

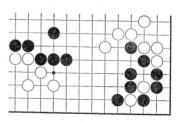

Problem 2

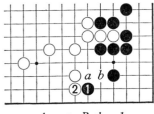

Ans. to Prob. 1

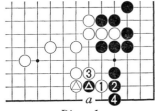

Dia. 1a

Answer to problem 1. Black can keep on with *a* or *b* after White 2, but even if he leaves the corner as it is, he has gained something from the exchange.

Dia. 1a. For example, suppose White later clamps him at 1. Leaving aside the possibility of drawing ▲ out at 3, Black can play 2 and then 4, which threatens Black *a* while preventing White 4. If he had somehow played ▲ after White 1 and 3, White would have answered at *a*, not ⬨, and Black 4 would not have worked.

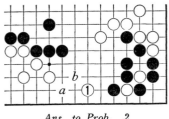

Ans. to Prob. 2

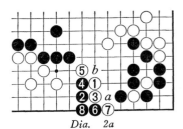

Dia. 2a

Answer to problem 2. White 1 is the best extension. Black cannot invade behind it: Black *a*, White *b*, for example.

Dia. 2a. If White extends on the third line, Black can invade at 2; after Black 8, if White connects at *a*, Black cuts at *b*. If White plays 1 too conservatively at 2 or 4, Black can counterextend to 3.

The Hitting-Under Tesuji

Dia. 1. When two stones oppose each other like ⊘ and ⬤ the diagonal move at 1 is a common endgame play, but it is well to remember that about half the time, as here, there is an even better play.

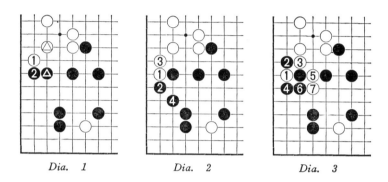

Dia. 1   Dia. 2   Dia. 3

Dia. 2. White should hit under the opposing stone with 1. He still keeps sente, and his result is at least two points better than in Dia. 1.

Dia. 3. If Black captures White 1, White can break through with 3, 5, and 7, and Black is going to lose more in the center than he has gained on the side.

Problem 1. White to play. What use can he make of his two stones in the corner?

Problem 2. Black to play. White might make the diagonal play in this position, but Black has a better move.

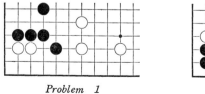

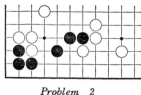

Problem 1   Problem 2

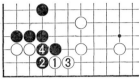

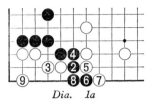

Ans. to Prob. 1   *Dia. 1a*

Answer to problem 1. White 1 threatens to revive the two stones in the corner, and Black has to defend with 2 and 4.

Dia. 1a. If he plays 2 here, White lives with 3 to 9.

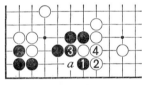

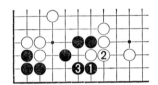

Ans. to Prob. 2   *Dia. 2a*

Answer to problem 2. Black should clamp at 1. He can connect at *a* after White 4, or he can leave the position unconnected. In the latter case he has still gained, because now *a* would be gote for White instead of sente.

Dia. 2a. If White wants sente badly enough, to make some other big play, he can connect solidly with 2, but then Black draws back to 3. This means a big local loss for White. Compare this result with Black's connecting at *a* in the correct answer, or with Black 1 at 3, White 2 at 1 in Dia. 2a.

On the First Line

Dia. 1. (next page) Black has an opportunity to make a four-point reverse sente play in the corner. What should it be?

— 86 —

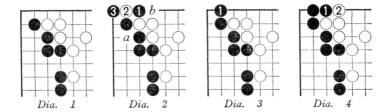

Dia. 1   Dia. 2   Dia. 3   Dia. 4

Dia. 2. This hane is wrong. It lets White make the throw-in at 2, which will force Black to connect eventually at *a*. Note that Black cannot play *b*, and that if White plays *b*, Black cannot connect at 2.

Dia. 3. The correct move is to descend straight to the edge with 1.

Dia. 4. Later Black can make this exchange in sente, so White's territory is the same as it was in Dia. 2, and Black's is from one to three points bigger.

This has been one example of defensive first-line technique. The next four problems are concerned with offensive first-line technique.

Problem 1. Black to play on the left edge. It would be wasteful of him simply to hane.

Problem 2. White to play.

Problem 3. Black to gain three points in sente.

Problem 4. White to play. It takes some reading out, but he has a much better play on the left edge than the hane.

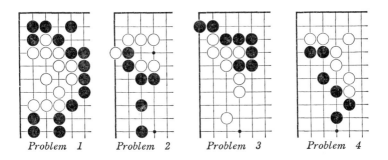

Problem 1   Problem 2   Problem 3   Problem 4

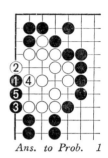

Ans. to Prob. 1

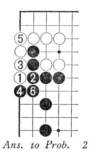

Ans. to Prob. 2

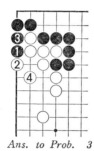

Ans. to Prob. 3

Answer to problem 1. Black can connect either up or down the edge.

Answer to problem 2. If Black plays 2 at 3, White cuts at 2.

Answer to problem 3. This is two points better for Black than playing 1 at 3.

Answer to problem 4. White can jump all the way in to 1. If he haned with 1 at 3, Black would answer at 1.

Dia. 4a. If Black wants to try to cut White off, he can only play 2 and 4 like this, but White 5 and 7 trap him in a shortage of liberties.

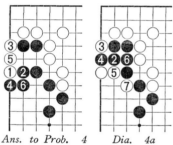

Ans. to Prob. 4   Dia. 4a

Placement Tesuji

Dia. 1. (next page) In this position White can hane at *a* in sente, but we are interested in what Black can do if he gets a chance to play first.

Dia. 2. He has an interesting placement tesuji at 1.

Dia. 3. If White blocks at 2, Black comes around with the hane at 3. If White tried to stop that at 5, Black would cut at 4, so White connects at 4 and Black plays 5. He need not connect at *a* (three points in reverse sente) after White 6. Even after White *a*, he has still gained about four points in comparison with White *a* in Dia. 1.

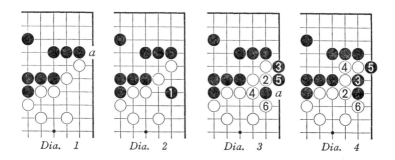

| Dia. 1 | Dia. 2 | Dia. 3 | Dia. 4 |

Dia. 4. Actually White 2 in this diagram is slightly better than 2 in the last diagram, but Black links up with 3 and 5. Once again, even without connecting (five points in gote) after White 6, he has made a profit.

Problem 1. White to play in the corner. The hane is the obvious move, but it gains in effect if preceded by a placement tesuji.

Problem 2. Black to play on the right side.

Problem 3. White to invade Black's territory.

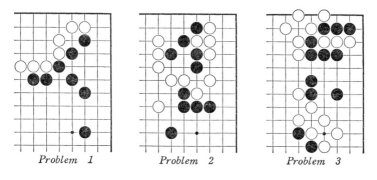

| Problem 1 | Problem 2 | Problem 3 |

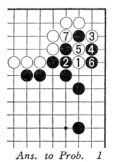

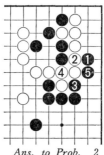

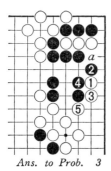

Ans. to Prob. 1   Ans. to Prob. 2   Ans. to Prob. 3

Answer to problem 1. White 1 and 3 are a standard combination. Black could reduce the damage somewhat by playing 4 at 5, (followed by White 4, Black 6), but then he would end in gote.

Answer to problem 2. If White plays 2 at 5, then Black 4, White 3, and Black 2 mean a disaster.

Answer to problem 3. White 1 threatens White *a*, which would save the three white stones and kill the three black stones in the corner. Black has to prevent this with 2, and White can link up with 3 and 5. White 1 at 2, followed by Black *a* and White 3, would be a failure, since Black could capture the invaders with a hane below 3.

Squeezing Tesuji

Dia. 1. White has a spectacular way to make use of the stone marked ⊘.

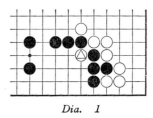

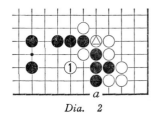

Dia. 1   Dia. 2

— 90 —

Dia. 2. He starts with this diagonal move, which is the eye-stealing tesuji with respect to both White ◯ and the coming white hane at *a*.

Dia. 3. Black's only answer is to give atari at 2. White gives a counter-atari at 3, squeezes with 5, and connects at 7. Black loses most of his territory and may even be in eye trouble.

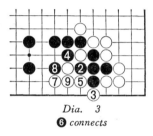

Dia. 3

❻ *connects*

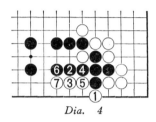

Dia. 4

Dia. 4. Playing the hane at White 1 would let Black take the key point with 2, and after that White could not do quite the same damage as in Dia. 3.

Problem 1. Black to play. If he uses his stranded stone to carry out a squeezing maneuver, he can reduce White's territory by a huge amount.

Problem 2. White to play. What can he do on the lower edge?

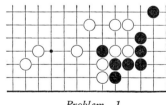

Problem 1

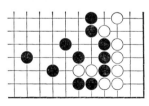

Problem 2

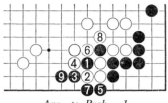

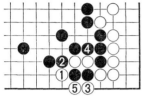

| Ans. to Prob. 1 | Ans. to Prob. 2 |

Answer to problem 1. Black sacrifices 1 in order to squeeze White with 3, 5, and 7. If he played 1 at 5, White would answer at 3.

Answer to problem 2. This sequence is clearly better than playing 1 at 3 and letting Black answer at 1.

The Monkey Jump

Dia. 1. When White has Black's territory undermined by a stone like ⊘ on the second line, he can reduce it by sliding in to 1. This move is called the monkey jump. There are various ways to answer it, but the one thing Black should not do is to give way and play *a*.

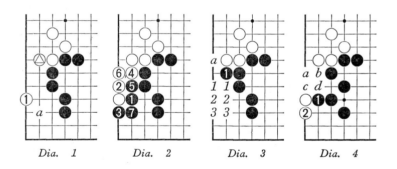

| Dia. 1 | Dia. 2 | Dia. 3 | Dia. 4 |

Dia. 2. In this particular position, the contact play at Black 1 is his best reply.

Dia. 3. The monkey jump in Dias. 1–2 gained nine points in sente as compared with Black 1 here. It reduced Black's territory by six and, since *a* is Black's sente, increased White's by three.

Dia. 4. With the position changed, Black 1 no longer works, but Black has a whole arsenal of other responses—at *a*, *b*, *c*, *d*, and even 2— to choose from. See problem 1.

Dia. 5. Here is a case where if White draws back at 3, he ends in gote, but this is wrong. Unless the enemy ignores it completely, the monkey jump should never lead to gote.

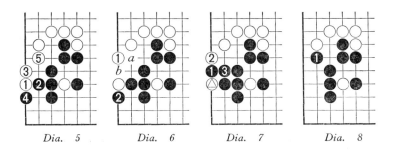

| *Dia.* 5 | *Dia.* 6 | *Dia.* 7 | *Dia.* 8 |

Dia. 6. To keep sente, White should jump back to 1 and ignore Black 2, leaving *a* and *b* as miai. His profit is only slightly less than in Dia. 5.

Dia. 7. He can also treat White ◯ as a forcing move and abandon it. If Black captures it, his profit is still two points less than—

Dia. 8. —if he had been allowed to play 1 here.

Problem 1. How should Black answer White's monkey jump? Two of the five moves suggested in Dia. 4 are correct.

Problem 2. White to answer Black's monkey jump. This one is harder to stop; only one move does the job properly.

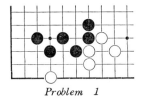

Problem 1

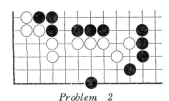

Problem 2

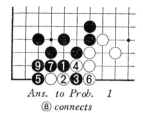

Ans. to Prob. 1

⑧ *connects*

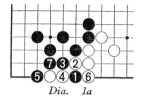

Dia. 1a

Answer to problem 1. Black 1 and the throw-in at 3 fit this shape nicely and keep White under control.

Dia. 1a. The order of Black 1 and 3 is reversible, and White can save the connection at 1 as a sente play for later.

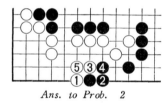

Ans. to Prob. 2

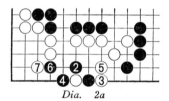

Dia. 2a

Answer to problem 2. White 1 halts Black in his tracks. If Black 2 at 3, White 5 would leave Black with gote.

Dia. 2a. Black cannot press forward with 2; his whole group dies.

Better than the Monkey Jump

The monkey jump is such a good move that it is easy to get into the habit of playing it automatically, but there are lots of times when another move is even better.

Dia. 1. (next page) Here it would definitely be a mistake. Black has a good reply to it at *a*, but he can also ignore it, since White has no very exciting follow-up move.

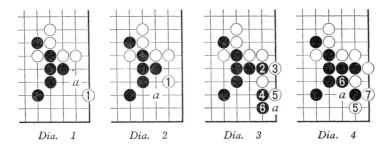

| Dia. 1 | Dia. 2 | Dia. 3 | Dia. 4 |

Dia. 2. The better play is to jump in on the second line to 1. When possible, this one-point jump is superior to the monkey jump nine times out of ten. If Black ignores it, White has a very big follow-up move at *a*.

Dia. 3. Here is one likely continuation. Even if Black has enough ko threats to play 6 at *a*, White still gets a better result than with the monkey jump because he more definitely ends in sente.

Dia. 4. If White has enough ko threats, he can also play 5 this way. If Black descends to 7 with 6, White *a* catches him in a snap-back.

Problems. In each a monkey jump on the first line would be possible, but there is a better move. See if you can find it. Black is to play in problems 1&2, White in 3&4.

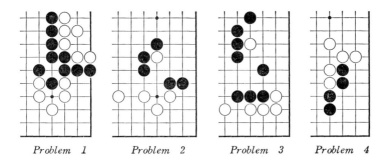

| Problem 1 | Problem 2 | Problem 3 | Problem 4 |

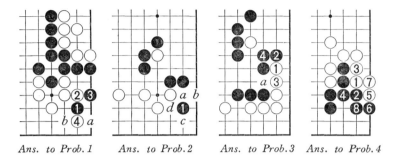

Ans. to Prob. 1   Ans. to Prob. 2   Ans. to Prob. 3   Ans. to Prob. 4

Answer to problem 1. Black can play 5 at *a* or, if he has the ko threats, at *b*.

Answer to problem 2. Adding to the effectiveness of Black 1 is the fact that White *a*, Black *b*, White *c*, Black *d* puts two white stones in atari.

Answer to problem 3. White 3 at *a* is a possible variation.

Answer to problem 4. This sequence works out to be two points better for White than the monkey jump.

Defending the Edge (I)

Dia. 1. How should Black answer White's hane at ◯? He would like to give atari at *a*, but White would then give a counter-atari at *b* and the result would be disastrous. Black is suffering from an empty triangle compounded by a shortage of liberties, so he must be prepared to retreat a little.

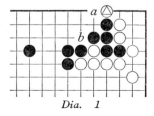

Dia. 1

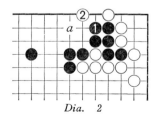

Dia. 2

Dia. 2. The next move to consider is drawing back at 1, but this makes horrible shape without really stopping White, who can jump out to 2. Black has to answer White 2 at *a*. White 2 is not the worst he has to fear, however, for White may play *a* instead of 2 and use that to attack his eye shape or mount an invasion of his entire upper side.

Dia. 3. The correct move is the diagonal connection, which makes excellent shape. Now Black is ready to block at *a*, if White lets him.

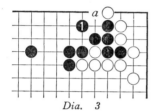

Dia. 3

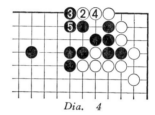

Dia. 4

Dia. 4. If White can do so in sente, he will carry on with 2 and 4; barring the unlikely case of his being able to play 3 at 4 and win the ko, Black cannot help giving up this much territory. At least he has kept his position strong and avoided getting into more serious trouble.

Problem 1. White to play. Counting a prisoner at the 2–4 point, he should be able to keep fifteen points of territory.

Problem 2. White to play. This time his goal is to keep twelve points of territory.

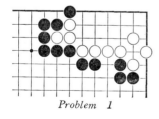

Problem 1

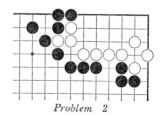

Problem 2

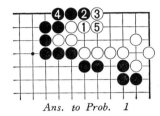

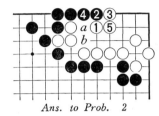

Ans. to Prob. 1

Ans. to Prob. 2

Answer to problem 1. White 1 at 2 is impossible—Black cuts at 1—and White 1 at 5 would let Black play 3 and cause an unnecessary two-point loss.

Answer to problem 2. White 1 is the only way to stop Black. After Black *a* and White *b*, White has twelve points left, counting a prisoner at the 2–4 point.

Defending the Edge (II)

Dia. 1. Once again the question is how to answer a white hane on the edge. Black cannot help giving way, but if he plays correctly, he can stop White from following up his hane in sente.

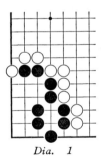

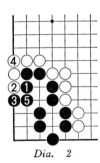

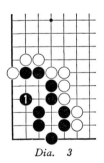

Dia. 1

Dia. 2

Dia. 3

Dia. 2. This Black 1 is a mistake, since White can play 2 and 4 in sente.

Dia. 3. The right move is this Black 1, the eye-protecting tesuji.

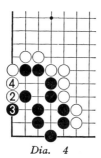

Dia. 4

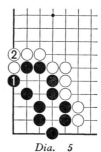

Dia. 5

Dia. 4. True, White can jump to 2 and reduce Black's territory by one more point than in Dia. 2, but White 2 and 4 are gote.

Dia. 5. More than likely White will not take gote to play as in Dia. 4, and Black will be able to block at 1 in sente. Now his corner is two points bigger than in Dia. 2.

Problem 1. Black to play and defend thirteen points of territory in sente. (He has captured one prisoner.)

Problem 2. White to play. Recall what Black's move would be in this position.

Problem 3. White to play. The obvious blocking move lets Black hane and connect in sente, so look for an alternative.

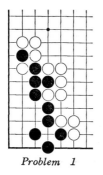

Problem 1

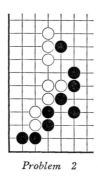

Problem 2

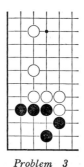

Problem 3

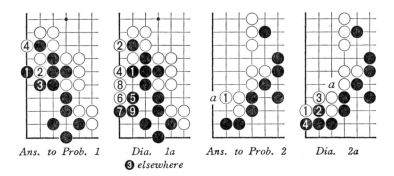

Ans. to Prob. 1   Dia. 1a   Ans. to Prob. 2   Dia. 2a

❸ elsewhere

Answer to problem 1. Black 1, threatening 4, is the right defense. It is also the point to which White would extend if Black failed to defend.

Dia. 1a. Giving atari at 1 and then playing elsewhere is the same as making no defense at all.

Answer to problem 2. White 1, taking the same point that Black would take, is the correct defense, although White *a* would be about equally good.

Dia. 2a. White 1 here is a mistake—White cannot connect after 4 because of Black *a*—and White 1 at 2 would be unthinkable.

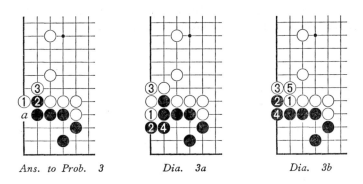

Ans. to Prob. 3   Dia. 3a   Dia. 3b

Answer to problem 3. After White 3, Black *a* would be gote.

Dia. 3a. Thus White gets to play 1 and 3 in sente.

Dia. 3b. If White plays 1 here, Black 2 and 4 are sente.

The Next Move

Dia. 1. There are times when you have to hold yourself to a smaller than possible immediate profit in order to prepare for a large next move. That is the case with White in this position.

Dia. 2. If he descends at 1, Black descends beside him at 2, then at 4, both times threatening to wedge in at 5 and capture.

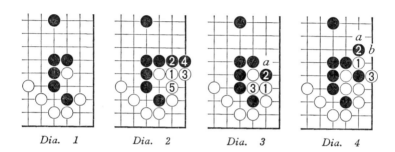

Dia. 1   Dia. 2   Dia. 3   Dia. 4

Dia. 3. He can do better if he holds himself to this White 1 initially. If Black connects at *a* after 3, White has sente.

Dia. 4. If Black does not connect, White can make this capture, which threatens a further move at *a* or *b*. The initial play in Dia. 3 was small, but the bonus it made possible in Dia. 4 is huge.

Problem 1. Black to play. If he restrains himself, he has a nice reverse-sente play on the lower edge.

Problem 2. White to play. How should be handle the lower side— with a large knight's move, a small knight's move, or a diagonal move?

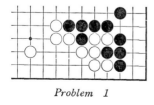

Problem 1

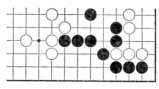

Problem 2

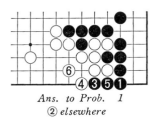

Ans. to Prob. 1
② elsewhere

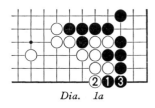

Dia. 1a

Answer to problem 1. Black should descend to 1, preparing for the tesuji at 3.

Dia. 1a. If he hanes with 1, he has no next move, and White's territory is two points larger.

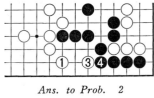

Ans. to Prob. 2
❷ elsewhere

Dia. 2a

Answer to problem 2. White 1 must precede White 3. If White played 3 first, Black could capture it by playing 1.

Dia. 2a. If White makes this small knight's move, he ends in gote with about five points less than in the correct answer.

Tesuji to Take Sente

Dia. 1. If Black neglects the left edge, White will hane at *a*. Black would like to prevent that, and if he plays correctly, he may be able to do so in sente. Can you see how?

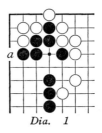

Dia. 1

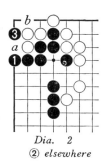 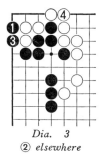 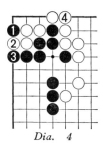

| Dia. 2 | Dia. 3 | Dia. 4 |
| ② elsewhere | ② elsewhere | |

Dia. 2. Good for you if you spotted the descent to Black 1, which is better than the hane at *a* because it gives Black the following jump to 3. If White wedges in between 1 and 3 at *a*, Black *b* starts a big ko. The only trouble with this is that if White simply ignores Black, both 1 and 3 are gote.

Dia. 3. Black's tesuji is to play 1 first. If White ignores that, Black can play 3 in sente.

Dia. 4. Accordingly, White will be more likely than in Dia. 2 to answer Black 1, allowing Black to descend to 3 in sente. If White tries to play 2 at 3, he runs afoul of the ko again.

Problem 1. White to defend the left edge in sente.

Problem 2. Black to defend the corner in sente.

Problem 3. White to play. He gets his largest profit by capturing the black stone, but that is gote. There is a way for him to handle the left edge in sente instead.

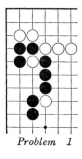 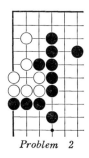 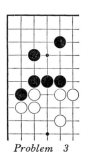

Problem 1   *Problem 2*   *Problem 3*

Answer to problem 1. White 1 and 3 are hard for Black to ignore, and they make the descent to 5 an atari. If Black plays 4 at *a*, White can turn elsewhere and Black cannot hane at 5. White 1 at 5 would threaten 1, but Black could ignore it, and then both White 5 and 1 would be gote.

Answer to problem 2. White 4 at 6, followed by Black 4 and White 1, is a possible variation. Black 1 at 3, followed by White 1 and Black *a*, would give Black more profit, but in gote.

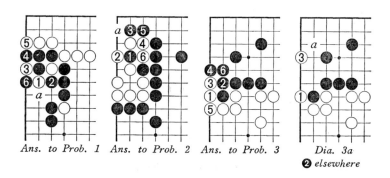

Ans. to Prob. 1   Ans. to Prob. 2   Ans. to Prob. 3   Dia. 3a
❷ *elsewhere*

Answer to problem 3. White 1 yields only three points less than capturing at 2 would do, so when sente is worth more than three points, it is correct.

Dia. 3a. If Black ignores White 1, White will not capture his stone but leap into the corner with 3. This is much bigger; next White can play *a*.

Sacrifice Tesuji

In the previous section we saw three examples of sacrifices made in order to take sente. In this section we shall see some sacrifices that actually yield profits as well as sente.

Dia. 1. (next page) White has to save two of his stones from being cut off.

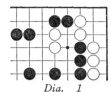

Dia. 1

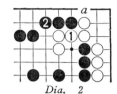

Dia. 2

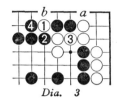

Dia. 3

Dia. 2. The obvious way to do this is to connect at 1. Black draws straight back with 2, instead of playing on the third line, so as to be able to hane at *a* in sente. By allowing this, White has not done his best.

Dia. 3. White's tesuji is to sacrifice 1, so that after 4 Black can no longer hane at *a*. That makes White's corner two points bigger than in Dia. 2, but the surprising thing is that Black's territory is also one point smaller. Black has been given one prisoner, but he has to play twice inside his own territory—at 4 and, later, *b*—to capture it.

Problem 1. Black to play on the right edge.

Problem 2. White to play on the right edge.

Problem 3. Black to play.

Problem 4. White to play. If he starts with a hane on the right edge, he loses one point.

Problem 1

Problem 2

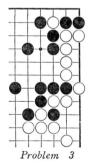

Problem 3

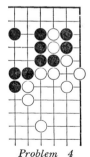

Problem 4

Answer to problem 1. Black 1 is a profitable sacrifice.

Dia. 1a. If White is allowed to connect at 2, then *a* becomes his sente and his territory is two points larger.

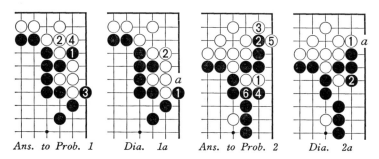

Ans. to Prob. 1   Dia. 1a   Ans. to Prob. 2   Dia. 2a

Answer to problem 2. White begins by playing 1 so that Black will have to capture two stones instead of just one.

Dia. 2a. If he blocks with 1, then since *a* is Black's sente, the corner is the same size as before, and Black's territory is two points larger.

Answer to problem 3. Black 1 at 7, White 1 would mean a two-point loss for Black.

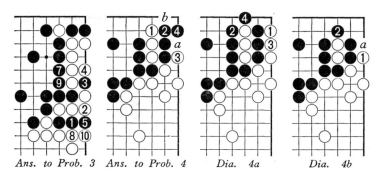

Ans. to Prob. 3   Ans. to Prob. 4   Dia. 4a   Dia. 4b

Answer to problem 4. Black 4 at *a*, White *b* would be a bad ko, and if Black omits 4—

Dia. 4a. White 1 and 3 gain three points in sente.

Dia. 4b. Since *a* is his sente, Black's territory is one point larger than in the correct answer.

Wedging Tesuji

The sacrifice tesuji of the previous section worked by forcing the enemy into a shortage of liberties. The tesujis of this section work in the same way.

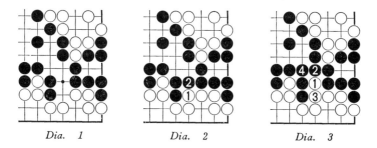

Dia. 1   *Dia. 2*   *Dia. 3*

Dia. 1.   White to play.

Dia. 2.   It would be rather thoughtless of him to treat this as a one-point-in-sente situation and push up with 1.

Dia. 3.   Instead, he should wedge in at 1. Black would be putting himself in atari if he played 2 at 3, so he has to give way with 2 and White gains three points in sente.

Problem 1.   Black to play. Find his tesuji and White's best answer to it.

Problem 2.   Black to play and defend his corner.

Problem 3.   White to play.

Problem 4.   White to play and reduce Black's territory by two points.

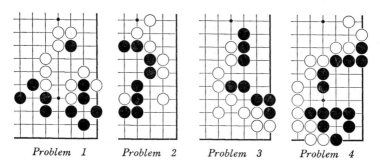

Problem 1   *Problem 2*   *Problem 3*   *Problem 4*

Answer to problem 1. White should answer at 2, not *a*, so as to end in sente.

Dia. 1a. If White cuts Black off with 2, he risks a big loss in a ko.

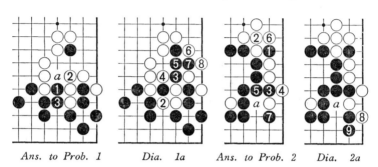

Ans. to Prob. 1	*Dia. 1a*	*Ans. to Prob. 2*	*Dia. 2a*

Answer to problem 2. Black 5 at *a* (ko) is worth considering, but even if Black has to give way with 5 and on through the next diagram, White is still haunted by a shortage of liberties.

Dia. 2a. He could not connect against Black *a*, for example.

Answer to problem 3. White 1 and 3 gain two points in sente. If Black does not connect at 4, White has a throw-in.

Dia. 3a. White 1 gains another two to four points.

Dia. 3b. This White 1 would gain only one point.

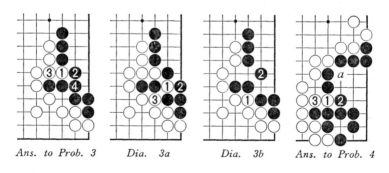

Ans. to Prob. 3	*Dia. 3a*	*Dia. 3b*	*Ans. to Prob. 4*

Answer to problem 4. White 1 threatens *a*. Black will have to connect at *a* later.

Capturing

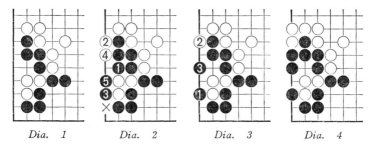

Dia. 1   Dia. 2   Dia. 3   Dia. 4

Dia. 1. How should Black capture the three white stones so as to get the greatest profit?

Dia. 2. This way gives him only seven points of territory: three prisoners plus the point marked ×.

Dia. 3. Black 1 and 3 are the right combination. They may be played in either order.

Dia. 4. After both sides have connected Black need make no further moves, so he has two points more than before.

Problem 1. Black to capture the two white stones.

Problem 2. Black to play. If he leaves this position alone, White can start a multi-step ko.

Problem 3. What is Black's best way to capture?

Problem 4. White to play and make seven points of territory by capturing three stones.

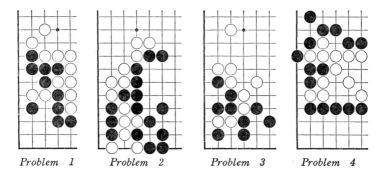

Problem 1   Problem 2   Problem 3   Problem 4

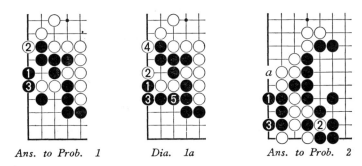

Ans. to Prob. 1   Dia. 1a   Ans. to Prob. 2

Answer to problem 1. After 3, Black will not have to fill any more liberties.

Dia. 1a. This hane gives him one or three points less profit, depending on whether White lets him capture 2 or not.

Answer to problem 2. After 1, if White opens the ko, Black makes an eye with 3. Black 1 also prepares for Black *a*.

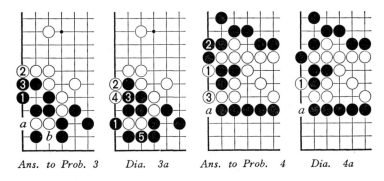

Ans. to Prob. 3   Dia. 3a   Ans. to Prob. 4   Dia. 4a

Answer to problem 3. Black's eye is safe. If White descends to *a*. Black *b* holds him in check.

Dia. 3a. This sequence loses Black four points.

Answer to problem 4. White 1 confronts Black with the choice of being captured at 2 or having White descend to 3, which makes White *a* destructive.

Dia. 4a. This hane gives White one less point of territory, and White *a* loses some of its force.

Dual-Purpose Moves

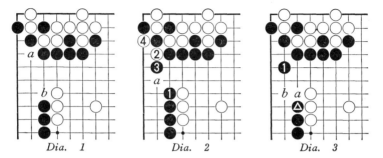

Dia.   1   Dia.   2   Dia.   3

Dia. 1. How should Black defend the left side, where White is threatening both *a* and, more seriously, *b*?

Dia. 2. If he plays the obvious 1, White can later capture with 2 and 4. Next White *a* is possible.

Dia. 3. The right move is this dual-purpose diagonal connection, which defends against both threats. The linkage between it and Black ● is unbreakable: White *a*, Black *b*, for example.

Problem 1. White to play on the left side.

Problem 2. Black to defend the left edge.

Problem 3. Black to play. How should he connect?

Problem 4. White to play on the left edge.

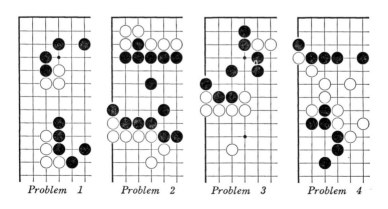

Problem   1   Problem   2   Problem   3   Problem   4

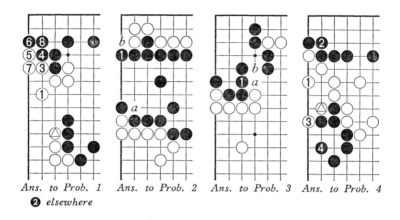

Ans. to Prob. 1   Ans. to Prob. 2   Ans. to Prob. 3   Ans. to Prob. 4

❷ elsewhere

Answer to problem 1. White 1 links across to ⊘ and enables White to play 3 to 7 in sente.

Answer to problem 2. Black 1 is two points better than Black *a*, one point because he can push out at *b* in sente and one point because he has not filled his territory unnecessarily at *a*.

Answer to problem 3. After White *a* and Black *b*, Black 1 will be in just the right place, giving Black the maximum amount of territory.

Answer to problem 4. White 1 threatens 2 while protecting White ⊘ from capture. If Black connects at 2, White can hane at 3 in sente.

Invasions

Dia. 1. (next page) Occasionally the enemy makes a mistake and gives you the chance to reduce one of his territories more than just slightly. This diagram shows a good example. Black is trying both to guard the cutting point at *a* and keep White from playing *b* in sente, and Black 1 would be an excellent dual-purpose move if it worked, but it does not.

Dia. 2. Black has seen that if White drives him down the edge, even the jumping-ahead tesuji at 5 cannot stop him from linking up with 6.

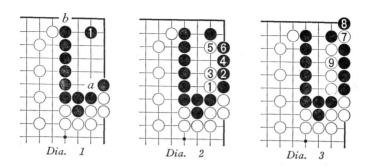

Dia. 1   Dia. 2   Dia. 3

Dia. 3. But he has forgotten about the throw-in at 7. If he catches himself in time, he will answer White 1 in Dia. 2 at the point between 3 and 5, but he still loses nearly half his territory.

Problem 1. White to invade Black's corner. The sequence involves a ko.

Problem 2. Black to invade White's corner—another ko.

Problem 3. Black to invade White's corner. Can White live?

Problem 4. White to play—a sort of one-two cut.

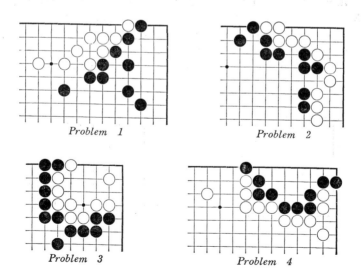

Problem 1   Problem 2

Problem 3   Problem 4

Answer to problem 1. If Black connects with 6, White 7 makes a living group. By playing 6 at *a*, Black can get a ko, but what he should have done before all this started was to draw back with ⬤ at 3.

Answer to problem 2. The ko is direct; Black can win it by connecting.

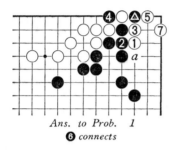

Ans. to Prob. 1

❻ connects

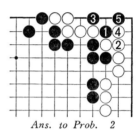

Ans. to Prob. 2

Answer to problem 3. Black 3 at 5 works, too. White should play 2 at 4, followed by Black 2 and White 3 or 5; then at least he can live.

Answer to problem 4. If Black plays 2 at 3 or 5, White extends to 2, gaining three liberties, then captures the two corner stones and kills the whole group. Note that White 1 at 3 would fail, Black answering at 5.

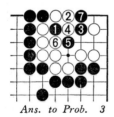

Ans. to Prob. 3

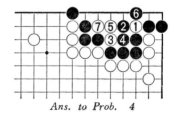

Ans. to Prob. 4

Tesuji that Attack Eye Shape

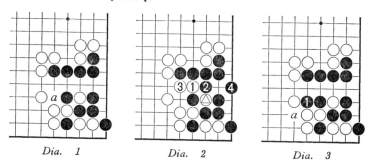

Dia. 1   Dia. 2   Dia. 3

Dia. 1. Even when an enemy group cannot be killed, it may be possible to earn a large profit by attacking it in the right way. That is certainly the case here.

What should White do? It would be a bad mistake for him to give atari at *a*.

Dia. 2. He should steal the eye at ◬ with 1 and 3. Black can still live, but White trims him down to three points of territory in sente.

Dia. 3. You can get an idea of the size of the moves in the previous diagram by comparing it with this one. Now Black has eight points of territory, and White has the cutting point at *a* to worry about.

Problem 1. Black to play. By threatening the group in the corner, he can make a tremendous invasion of the area to the left.

Problem 2. White to play. If he attacks the group on the lower side in the right way he can capture part of it in sente.

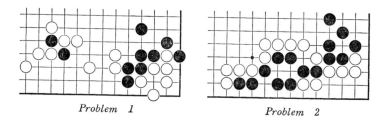

Problem   1   Problem   2

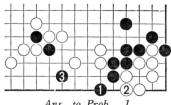

Ans. to Prob. 1

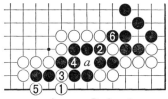

Ans. to Prob. 2

Answer to problem 1. Black 1 threatens 2 and a ko; if White connects at 2, Black can jump all the way in to 3.

Answer to problem 2. If Black plays 2 at 3, White *a*, Black 4, and White 2 kill him, and Black 2 at *a*, White 3 would mean a life-or-death ko. White 1 at *a*, Black 4, White 2, Black 1, and White *a* is another possibility, but it ends in White's gote.

Miscellaneous Tesuji

There are many, many other positions in which the right tesuji will yield a little extra profit. Here are a few of them.

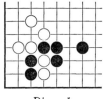

Dia. 1

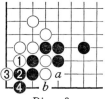

Dia. 2

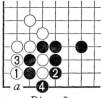

Dia. 3

Dia. 1. White has lost two stones, but he can use them to squeeze Black in sente. How should he start?

Dia. 2. If he turns in at 1, Black can block with 2, then answer White 3 by descending to 4. Later, as White connects, he will capture with *a* and *b*.

Dia. 3. White can get a bigger share of the corner if he starts with 1 in this diagram. After 4 Black's territory is one point smaller than in Dia. 2 and White's is, if we average White *a* and Black *a*, two (−) points larger.

Problem 1. Black to play. Connecting above or pushing under the white stone on the 2–4 point is not good enough.

Problem 2. White to play. This shape resembles the example of Dias. 1 to 3.

Problem 3. White to play. Just turning at the 4–5 point would be sente, but there is a better sente play.

Problem 4. Black to play and reduce White's territory in the diagram to ten points while making a little territory for himself.

Problem 5. White to play. How should he defend his holdings in the center?

Problem 6. Black to play. A mere hane on the lower edge would be far too kind to White.

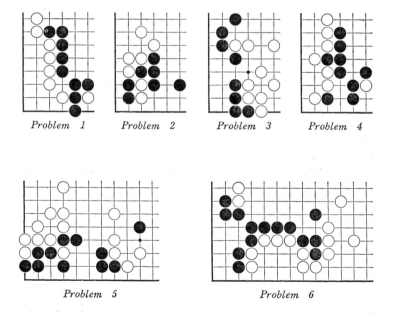

Problem 1   Problem 2   Problem 3   Problem 4

Problem 5   Problem 6

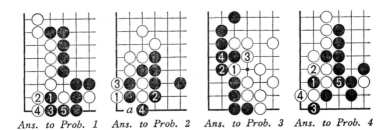

Ans. to Prob. 1　　Ans. to Prob. 2　　Ans. to Prob. 3　　Ans. to Prob. 4

Answer to problem 1. Black 1 (four points in gote), is better than 1 at 5 (one point in sente).

Answer to problem 2. If Black plays 2 at 3, White 3 at *a* makes a big, one-sided ko.

Answer to problem 3. Black cannot fight this one-sided ko, so he may as well connect at 4. Black 2 at 3, White 2 would lose him the corner.

Answer to problem 4. Black 1 threatens Black 2, so White has to connect there and let Black earn the maximum.

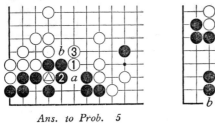

Ans. to Prob. 5　　　　　Ans. to Prob. 6

Answer to problem 5. White 1 takes advantage of the stone marked ⊘. If Black answers at *a*, White can give atari at *b*, then turn elsewhere.

Answer to problem 6. Black 1, the eye-stealing tesuji, cannot be captured—White 2 at *a*, Black 3, for example, or White 4 at 5, Black *b*, White *a*, Black 4—so White's best course is to connect at 2 and 4 and make Black link up in gote with 3 and 5.

Cut, Clamp, or Hane?

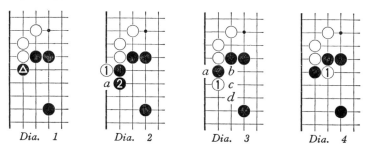

Dia. 1   Dia. 2   Dia. 3   Dia. 4

Dia. 1. During the endgame, when a stone like Black ● is unprotected by any direct form of connection, there are generally three moves for White to consider.

Dia. 2. If nothing else works, White can always hane at 1 and Black will have to give way at 2. If he blocks at *a*, White can cut at 2 and start a dangerous (for Black) ko.

Dia. 3. Much more effective is the clamping tesuji. If Black descends to *a*, White must be ready with a counter-move at, for example, *b*, *c*, or *d*.

Dia. 4. Most effective of all, when it cannot be captured, is the direct cut.

Problems. In each the question is whether to cut, clamp, or hane, except that in problem 3 'push out' replaces 'cut'. White to play in 1 & 4, Black to play in 2 & 3.

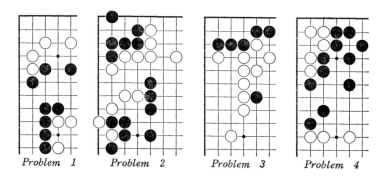

Problem 1   *Problem 2*   *Problem 3*   *Problem 4*

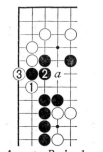 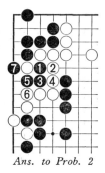 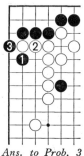

Ans. to Prob. 1   Ans. to Prob. 2   Ans. to Prob. 3

Answer to problem 1.   Black connects solidly at 2 so as to give himself the option of taking sente after 3. White 1 at 2 would not work, because Black would give atari at *a*.

Answer to problem 2.   If White plays 2 at 5, Black 4 leaves the whole side dead.

Answer to problem 3.   Clamping at 1 gives Black the most profit. If he played at 2 or 3 instead, White would reply at 1.

Dia. 3a.   White can preserve some of his territory in sente, but at the loss of a stone.

Answer to problem 4.   White can only hane at 1.

Dia. 4a.   If he clamps, he ends up trading his corner for a small gain on the side.

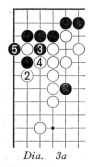 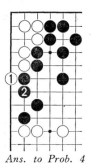 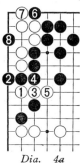

Dia.   3a   Ans.   to Prob.   4   Dia.   4a

Hane or Descent?

Dia. 1.   (next page) In this type of position, whether to hane or descend on the right side can be a difficult problem.

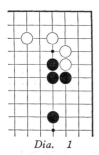

Dia. 1

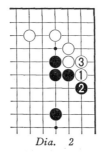

Dia. 2

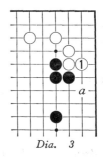

Dia. 3

Dia. 2. The hane gives more profit, but tends to be gote, unless White can follow it with a cut or clamp.

Dia. 3. The descent gives a smaller profit than the hane if answered, but a larger profit if Black ignores it and lets White jump in to *a*.

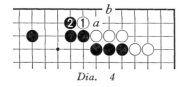

Dia. 4

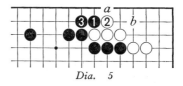

Dia. 5

Dia. 4. Another possibility is to play the hane as a forcing move, as White is doing here, and not connect immediately at *a*. If Black cuts at *a*, White has a good defense at *b*.

Dia. 5. If Black hanes at 1 first, White has to defend at 2, not *a*, and after 3 Black can hane again at *a*, forcing White to give way to *b*.

Problem 1. Black to play: hane or descent? One of the two is automatically correct in this position.

Problem 2. White to play: ditto.

Problem 3. Black to play: ditto.

Problem 4. White to play: ditto.

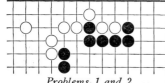

Problems 1 and 2

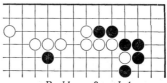

Problems 3 and 4

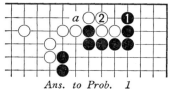

Ans. to Prob. 1

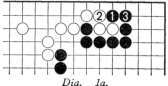

Dia. 1a.

Answer to problem 1. Black descends in sente to 1. White's best answer is to connect solidly at 2. Later, he will have to connect again at *a*.

Dia. 1a. If Black hanes, he gets only about one point more of profit than before, and in gote instead of sente.

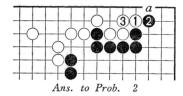

Ans. to Prob. 2

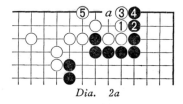

Dia. 2a

Answer to problem 2. First of all, White should hane at 1. Connecting at 3 gives him *a* to play next, but it would also be good for him to play just the 1–2 exchange as a forcing maneuver to keep Black from descending to 1 in sente.

Dia. 2a. Suppose White descends with 1. If he does not continue at 3, a black atari at 3 gives him a slightly worse result than if he had let Black play first—if Black descended to 2, White would not answer at 1—but White 3 is gote, since Black 4 threatens to capture four stones with *a*. That is also the reason White cannot play 3 at 4. If he is going to end in gote anyway, the correct answer gives him more profit.

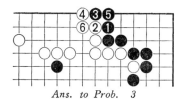

Ans. to Prob. 3

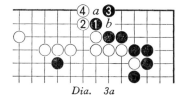

Dia. 3a

Answer to problem 3. In this position the correct move for either side is to descend. Black 3 and 5 are sente.

Dia. 3a. Suppose Black hanes. If White omits 4, Black is stuck with gote, while if White plays 4, Black gets only the same profit as before, (assume White *a*, Black *b*). That means that the hane may be worse than descending and cannot be better.

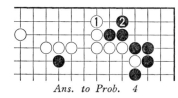

Ans. to Prob. 4

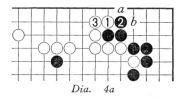

Dia. 4a

Answer to problem 4. If Black answers White 1, then 2 is the proper point, (although a jump down to the first line would probably come to the same thing). If Black does not answer, then White will jump forward to 2 himself.

Dia. 4a. Now White has gote, and White *a*, Black *b* etc. will yield him less than White 1, Black elsewhere, White 2 would in the correct answer diagram. If White wanted the result in Dia. 4a, he could get it by continuing from the correct answer. That in itself is enough to remove the hane at 1 from serious consideration.

CHAPTER 4

The Macroendgame

The preceding two chapters have been concerned with what might be called the microendgame, that is, with fairly small, localized situations. This chapter looks at the macroendgame, (in Japanese the *oyose*), where the moves are larger, precise counting is more difficult, and the board must be considered as a whole. The macroendgame has much in common with the middle game, and it is partly governed by middle-game strategy: attack weak enemy groups to make profit in sente; defend weak friendly groups before your opponent attacks them; don't chase your opponent into your own potential territory; etc. Perception is important, too. You have to see the crucial weaknesses in one side's position that give the other side large moves. These weaknesses, which often amount to invasion points, may not be obvious, but they are what the endgame should really be all about.

Nine macroendgame problems follow, with five possible answers marked *A* to *E* in each. Mark down your choice, then turn the page. Each answer is evaluated and a scoring chart is provided at the end of the chapter.

Problem 1

White to play

This problem comes from a game in a ladies' professional tournament. Of the five moves shown, one is very large, three are of moderate size, and one is a mistake.

Your choice	

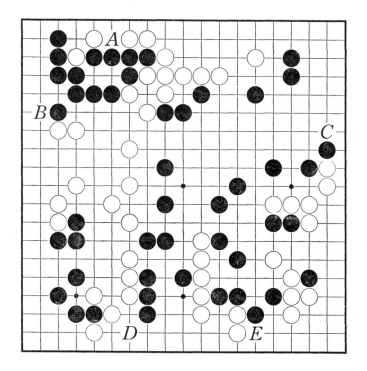

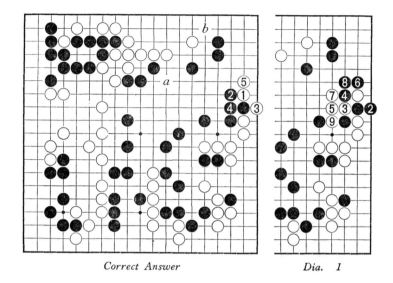

Correct Answer   Dia. 1

Correct answer: C (10 points). This clamping tesuji cuts Black's biggest territory in half. White has other good moves at *a*, (which could lead to an exchange of most of Black's center territory for most of White's upper side territory), and *b* to play next, and she can hardly lose. If Black descends to 2 in Dia. 1, White cuts at 3.

D (8 points). Although White 1 in Dia. 2 on the next page is not an urgent move, it is still big because it enables White to jump into the corner at *a*. Black will probably answer at 2 and 4 in Dia. 3, then go to the upper right, planning to meet White *a* with Black *b*. White 1 has some additional value in that it enables White to link up with her group to the right, but that will not actually yield much territory if Black plays *c*, White *d*, Black *e* in sente first.

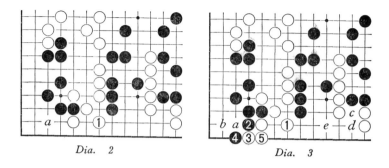

Dia. 2

Dia. 3

A (*6 points*).   Compare Dias. 4 and 5 below. If Black answers White 1 in Dia. 4 at *a*, White has gained nine points in sente. White or Black *a* is worth six points in gote (you should verify these figures). White or Black 1 is thus worth $9+(1/2\times6)=12$ points in gote, but twelve points in gote are nothing when compared with the correct answer.

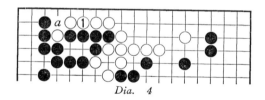

Dia. 4

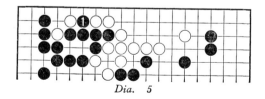

Dia. 5

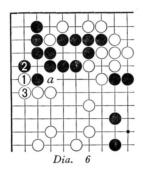

Dia. 6

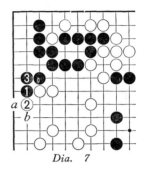

Dia. 7

B (4 points). White 1 in Dia. 6 is worth about nine points, White *a* being sente later. Note that if Black hanes here, as in Dia. 7, her continuation is Black *a*, White *b*. She cannot cut at the right of 2 or clamp at *b*.

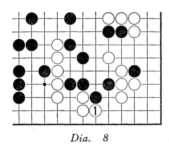

Dia. 8

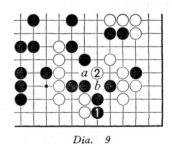

Dia. 9

E (2 points). White 1 in Dia. 8 may not be completely worthless, but why play it? If Black descends to 1 in Dia. 9. White responds with 2, threatening *a* and *b*, thus capturing Black 1 and two other stones.

The clamping play of the first problem is an exceedingly destructive tesuji, but the next problem contains some even larger moves. It is taken from a game between two nine-dans. The board is still rather open, for the endgame has just begun.

Problem 2

White to play

Your choice	

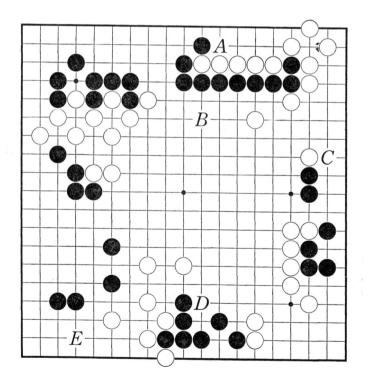

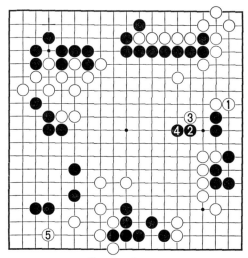

Correct Answer

Correct answer: C (10 points). White 1 is best not only because of its direct territorial value, but also because it attacks the eye space of the black group on the right side. If Black defends by running out with 2 and 4, White has sente to take the next biggest point at 5. If Black does not defend, White can attack at 3 and contain Black in sente, building toward a large center territory.

E (8 points). White 1 in Dia. 1 on the facing page is quite large, and it gives eye space to a somewhat unsettled white group, but Black will ignore it and play 2. White can then jump from 1 to *a*, but that does not make up for the loss he has suffered on the right side.

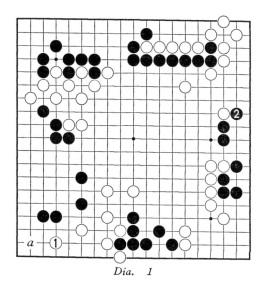

Dia. 1

A (6 points). White 1 in Dia. 2 works out to be worth about twelve points in gote. If Black connects at a, White has gained about six points in sente, as compared with Dia. 3, and White a would be worth another twelve points in gote: $6+(\frac{1}{2}\times12)=12$. White 1 does not attack or defend any weak groups, however, and its value is far below that of the previous two answers.

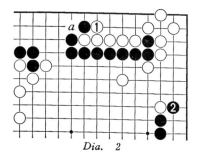

Dia. 2

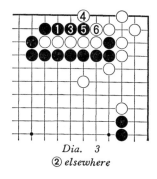

Dia. 3
② elsewhere

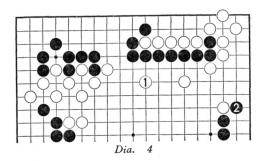

Dia. 4

B (4 points). White 1 in Dia. 4 is not really a good move. It comes too close to the solid Black wall above, and there is ample danger of Black's being able to break through around it in the future. Black will reply at 2, of course.

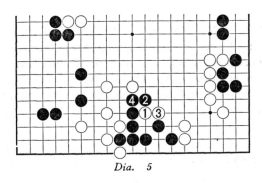

Dia. 5

D (2 points). White 1 in Dia. 5 is a bad overplay. It reduces Black to one eye, but at the same time it weakens the adjacent white group to the left. Between defending that group and hanging on to 1 and 3, White has no real chance of killing Black. The only result of this attack, then, will be to drive Black into the center and spoil the potential territory that White had there.

Moves like the correct answer in the previous problem, that attack an enemy group's eye shape and take a large profit at the same time, are never bad. They are almost always to be preferred to large moves that do not attack, or to attacking moves like the ones in Dia. 5 on the facing page that do not make any direct profit.

In the next problem neither player has much chance of making territory in the center, so the choices are all at the edges.

Problem 3

Black to play

Your choice	

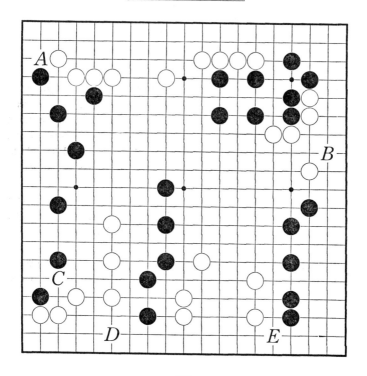

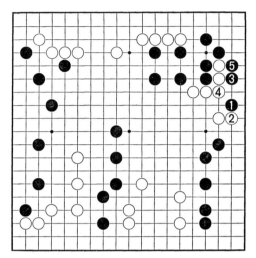

Correct Answer

Correct answer: B (10 points). Black 1, 3, and 5 are a tesuji combination that you should know. (If White plays 4 at 5, Black plays 5 at 4). What makes them the best answer is not so much the profit at the edge as the fact that they leave White with uncertain eye shape. White will have to go on the defensive, and Black should be able to make additional profit out of attacking him. Black has the initiative.

E (8 points). Black 1 in Dia. 1 on the next page will be met by a similar diagonal move at 2. White has defended his major weakness and has some chance of taking over the initiative in the game.

A (6 points). The ⬣-⬡ exchange has somewhat reduced the value of Black 1 in Dia. 2. White will respond with the same diagonal move as before.

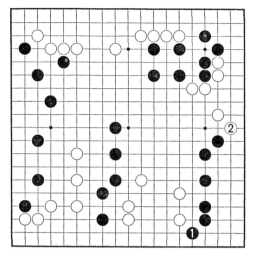

Dia. 1

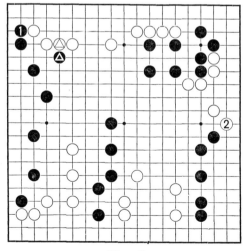

Dia. 2

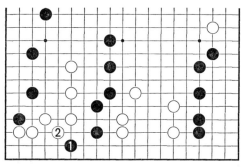

Dia. 3

D (*4 points*).   Black 1 in Dia. 3 may be sente, but 2 gives this white group plenty of eye shape. In the correct answer Black's invasion left White much more unstable.

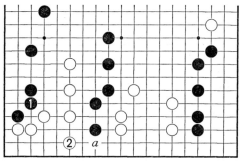

Dia. 4

C (*2 points*).   Black 1 in Dia. 4 is inferior to Black 1 in Dia. 3. White will defend by jumping down to 2, and next he can cross under at *a*.

The correct answers in the two preceding problems were correct because they attacked profitably. The key word is 'profitably'. Attack and defense can be extremely important in the macroendgame, but it is well to remember that there can also be such a thing as an unprofitable attack, or an unnecessary defense.

Problem 4

Black to play

Your choice

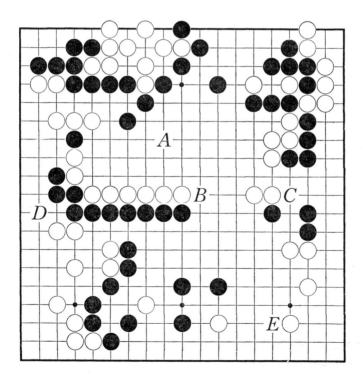

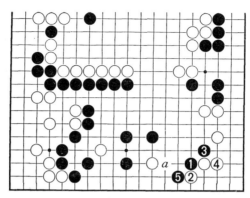

Correct Answer

Correct answer: E (10 points). Although the continuation is a bit difficult,* there is no question that Black 1 is the right move. White's strongest resistence is with 2, but after White 4 either Black 5 or Black *a* is possible. Black 5 gives the result shown in Dia. 1 below, and Black makes a large profit by swallowing up White's extension marked ◯. She has had to sacrifice three of her own stones, but three stones are only six points; Black *a* holds the loss to exactly that. If White plays 8 as in Dia. 2, Black can push through at 9, and White cannot then play *a* because of Black *b* etc.

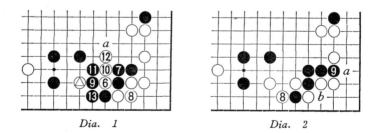

Dia. 1   *Dia. 2*

* I missed it, failing to answer White 4. This problem is from one of my own games. —Ogawa

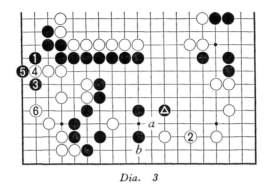

Dia. 3

D (*8 points*). Black 1 in Dia. 3 is big, but not really urgent. A white move at 1 would be gote, since Black does not have any territory to speak of on the left side to defend. White will seize the chance to play 2, threatening *a* and *b*. (White *a* would lead to the capture of Black ⬤).

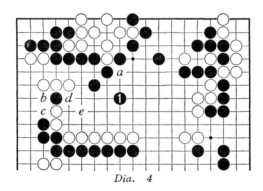

Dia. 4

A (*6 points*). Black 1 in Dia. 4 is valuable in that it defends the cutting point at *a*. It also prepares for Black *b*—without 1, White could answer Black *b* with *c*, but after 1 he has to play *d*, Black *c*, White *e*. In spite of that, White will ignore Black 1 and go to the lower right corner.

C (4 points). Black 1 in Dia. 5 is unnecessary; the black group is safe without it. Note that *a* is Black's sente. If White attacks with *b*, then after Black *c* and White 1, Black can even afford to play *d*.

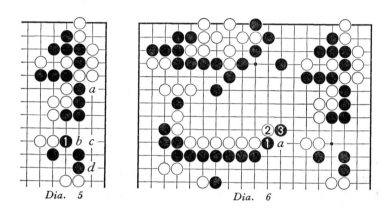

Dia. 5   Dia. 6

B (2 points). Black 1 in Dia. 6 is an overplay. Black would be accomplishing nothing if she played 3 at *a* and let White play 3, but Black 3 is a failure, as the continuation in Dia. 7 below shows. White 16 captures Black's cutting stone. (Black *a*, White *b*).

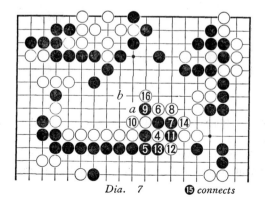

Dia. 7   ⑮ *connects*

Contact plays against a knight's-move corner enclosure are frequently effective. In addition to the answer to the previous problem, recall the examples on pages 17 and 24 in chapter 1.

Problem 5

Black to play

Your choice	

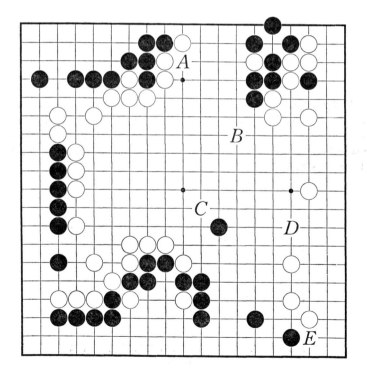

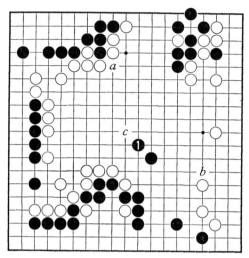

Correct Answer

Correct answer: C (10 points). Black 1 may not look like much, but besides reducing White's large center, it prepares for a cut at *a*, an attachment at *b* (or perhaps a deeper invasion), etc., and gives Black excellent overall prospects. White almost has to defend at *c*, so Black 1 is a sente move.

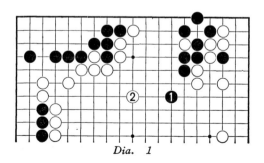

Dia. 1

B (*8 points*).   Black 1 in Dia. 1 at the bottom of the previous page is also an extension into the center, but it is actually somewhat off center. White will be glad for the chance to defend at 2.

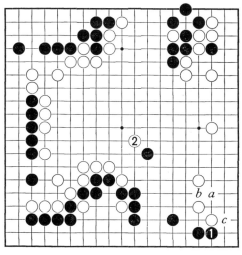

Dia.   2

E (*6 points*).   This crawling move is always big—it aims at Black *a*, White *b*, Black *c*—but here White 2 is much bigger. The center simply cannot be ignored.

D (4 points). Black 1 in Dia. 3 is a bad move. The sequence up to 4 may be sente for Black, but its main effect is to solidify White's hold on the right side. Black 3 at 4 might be better, but the fighting that leads to is not particularly favorable either. If Black is going to play here, he should find some better starting point, such as *a* or *b*.

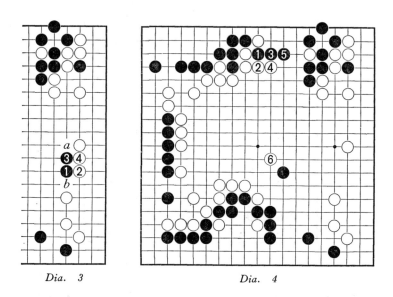

Dia. 3   Dia. 4

A (2 points). Black 1 in Dia. 4 gives Black gote at the worst possible time, actually helping White to make territory in the center. Black's territorial gain on the upper side is negligible.

As this last problem showed, a very big move can look rather small until it is tested against the enemy's playing there. Try that test on the next problem, too.

Another lesson to be learned from the last problem is not to extend too deeply into a large center territory. Small, solid extensions are better than large, loose ones that can be cut through.

Problem 6

Black to play

Your choice	

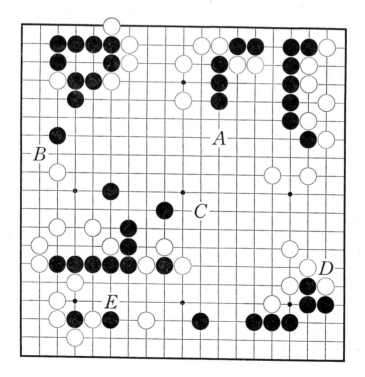

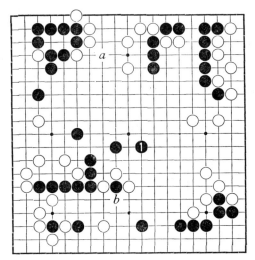

Correct Answer

Correct answer: C (*10 points*). Black 1 is a multi-purpose move: it strengthens a weak black group; it reduces White's territorial prospects to the right; it aims to attack the white group on the upper side at *a*; and it threatens Black *b*. White would like to play 1 himself if he could.

D (*8 points*). Black 1 and 3 in Dia. 1 on the next page are large, and there is some chance that Black may be able later to clamp at *a*, (if White descends to *b*, Black plays *c*, White *d*, Black *e*). White, however, will force Black at 4, then take the key point at 6, forestalling Black *a*, attacking the black center group, and surrounding a large territory.

B (*6 points*). The diagonal move in Dia. 2 is not bad, but it affects only territory, lacking any offensive or defensive significance. White can ignore it because he is linked up at ⊘, and similarly Black could ignore White 1.

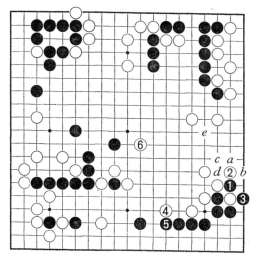

Dia. 1

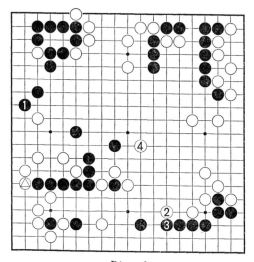

Dia. 2

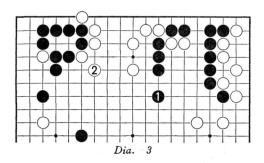

Dia. 3

A (4 points). Black in Dia. 3 is jumping into a largely neutral area. White will probably welcome the opportunity to defend his upper-side group with 2.

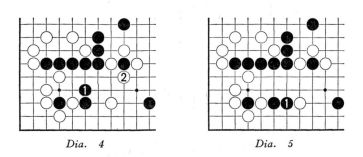

Dia. 4   *Dia. 5*

E (2 points). Black 1 in Dia. 4 is a mistake. If White replies at 2, for instance, he has by far the best of the exchange. A better idea, although a risky one, would be for Black to play 2 himself. If he is determined to rescue his stone on the lower side, then 1 in Dia. 5, not 1 in Dia. 4, is the proper way to do so.

The last two problems should have demonstrated that large macro-endgame moves can occur in the center. More often, however, they occur at the sides, as in the next problem.

Problem 7

Black to play

Your choice	

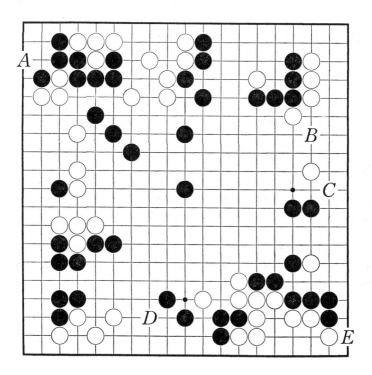

— 149 —

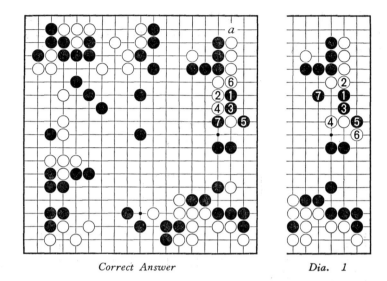

Correct Answer   Dia. 1

Correct answer: B (*10 points*). All the other choices pale in comparison to the invasion at 1. Black is not just reducing or enlarging territory; he is stealing territory from White and making it his own. He is also cutting into White's eye space, and next he can hane at *a* in sente.

If White connects at 2 in Dia. 1, Black should run head-on into his stone with 3. He can get out past White 4 with the hane at 5 and jump to 7, a standard tesuji combination.

E (*8 points*). Although not a large move, the hane at 1 in Dia. 2 on the facing page can be played in sente right now. If White ignored it, his group could easily die.

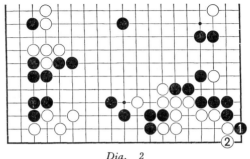

Dia. 2

D (*6 points*). Black 1 in Dia. 3 below gives eye shape to the black group on the lower side, but it does not pose any serious threat to the white group to the left, so White will ignore it to play 2 to 6 on the right side in sente.   After this, Black's chance to invade is gone, and his prospects in this handicap game are not good.   Black 1 at *a* would be a better move on the lower side, but still not up to the correct answer.

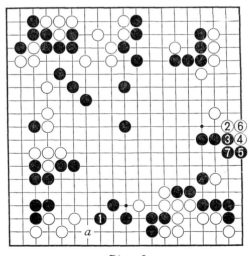

Dia. 3

A (*4 points*). Black 1 in Dia. 4 is worth about eleven points, but it does not threaten anything, nor is it necessary for the safety of the black group, which is connected to the center.

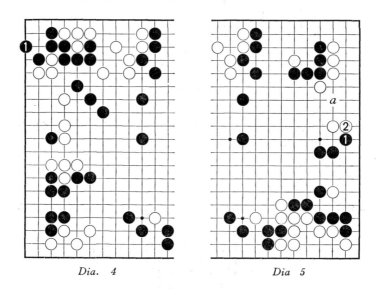

Dia. 4   Dia 5

C (*2 points*). Black 1 in Dia. 5 is the kind of sente move that one should not make, because it destroys the better invasion sequence starting with Black *a*.

The intrinsic bigness of an invasion like the one in the previous problem cannot be overemphasized. Bear also in mind the size of a defensive move that prevents such an invasion.

The next two problems are quite hard.

Problem 8

Black to play

Your choice	

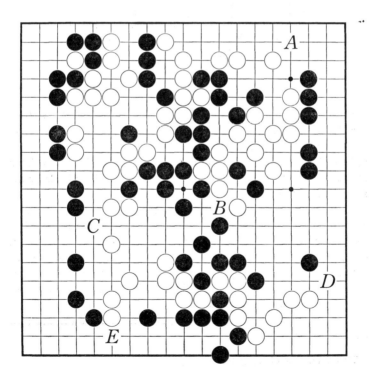

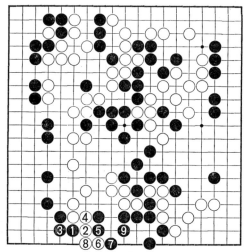

Correct Answer

Correct answer: E (10 points). Black 1 resolves what has been
a rather delicate situation involving the corner and the black group
on the lower side.   After defending both places with the sequence to
9, Black has nearly sixty points on the left and lower sides alone. That
is equal to all of White's territory put together, so Black leads by the
margin of her* right side and center territory.

If Black does not defend here, White will probe at the corner with
1 and 3 in Dia. 1 on the next page. If Black answers with 2 and 4,
White will shift and attack the group on the lower side with 5.   Black
can just barely live by making the throw-in at 12, but White gets to
play 9 and 15 in sente, which means that he can live in the corner by
connecting at 19.   (If Black *a*, White *b*, or if Black *b*, then White *a*,
Black *c*, White *d*).   Black has already lost more than twenty points
as compared with the correct answer, and she still has the clamp at
e left to worry about.

* This is another of my games.   —Ogawa

If Black answers White 1 by descending to 2 in Dia. 2, White will live on the left side with 3 and 5, and of course *a* will still be his sente, threatening the group to the right.

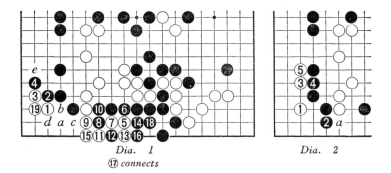

Dia. 1

⑰ *connects*

Dia. 2

A (8 points).   Black 1 in Dia. 3 is certainly a big move—the difference between it and White 1 in Dia. 4 is almost twenty points—and it secures ample eye space for the group on the right side, which is another plus factor, but it is not as big as the defense of the lower left corner.

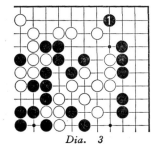

Dia. 3

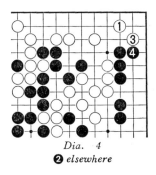

Dia. 4

❷ *elsewhere*

D (*6 points*).   Black 1 and 3 in Dia. 5 are also big, but less so than the upper right and lower left corners.   In those areas either side could make territory; here only Black can do so.   Black 1 is not a double sente point.   It is worthless without 3, and White would not play 1 himself, but rather *a*, or some move around 3.

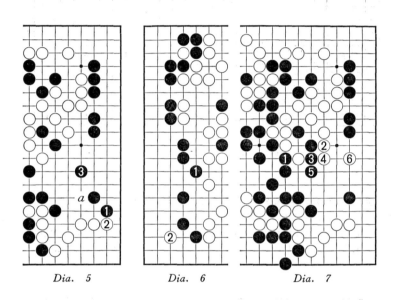

Dia. 5   Dia. 6   Dia. 7

C (*4 points*).   Black 1 in Dia. 6 covers a thin spot in the black line, but leaves the corner open.   White could not break through here even without Black 1.

B (*2 points*).   Black 1 in Dia. 7 seems to be prompted by unnecessary fear for the safety of the center group.   The exchange of 1 for 2 causes Black a loss.   She can no longer draw out her stones with 3 and 5 without having White invade the right side at 6.

The preceding problem showed the importance of foreseeing disaster before it occurs. A good player's attention is aroused just as much by defects in his own positions as by weaknesses in his opponent's positions.

This next problem is the last of the chapter.

Problem 9

White to play

Your choice	

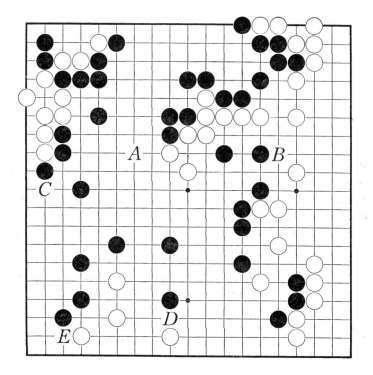

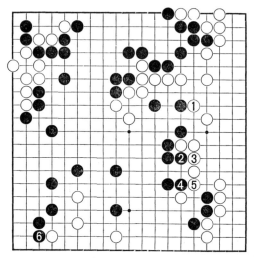

Correct Answer

Correct answer: B (10 points). White is perhaps a bit behind in this game, from one of the professional tournaments, but if he fails to defend at 1, he drops out of competition altogether. The reason is that Black is threatening the attachment and cross-cut shown in Dia. 1 on the facing page, which would break up White's only large territory. If White plays 2 at 3, Black can play *a* in sente, then 2. Following the cross-cut, if White gives atari at 4 in Dia. 2, Black gives a counter-atari at 5 and connects at 7. If White plays 4 in Dia. 3, Black can break through with 5 and 7 and, if cut off by White 10, live with 11 and 13.

E (8 points). White 1 in Dia. 4 is a strong second-best. After White 1 in the correct answer diagram, Black made two forcing moves, then played here himself with 6.

If Black answers 1 at *a* in Dia. 4, White has made a big profit in sente. In this game Black will ignore White 1 to play on the right side, however, as in Dia. 1.

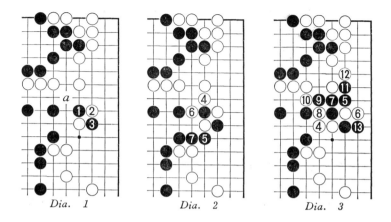

Dia. 1   Dia. 2   Dia. 3

Let's take this opportunity to go through some of the follow-up
moves to White 1 in Dia. 4. White *a* and White *b* are two possibilities,
but there is also the peep-and-hane combination shown in Dia. 5.
Black 4 is the simplest way to answer them; next *a* is the correct point
for either side. Black 4 in Dia. 6 is also possible, and Black can
defend his territory by playing 6 as shown there, or he can shift 6 to
the right and play for the exchange shown in Dia. 7, cutting off the
stones marked ◯. Whichever variation he chooses, however, he
cannot avoid a sizable loss.

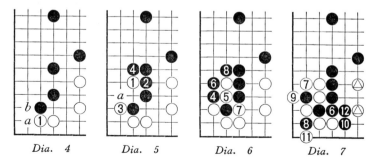

Dia. 4   Dia. 5   Dia. 6   Dia. 7

— 159 —

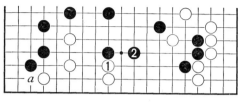

Dia. 8

D (*6 points*). White 1 in Dia. 8 is much smaller than White *a* would be. If Black answers at 2, White has gained rather little. He might actually prefer to play from the direction of 2 himself, instead of 1.

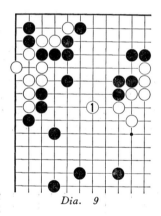

Dia. 9

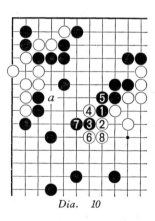

Dia. 10

A (*4 points*). White 1 in Dia. 9 is smaller than it looks; even if Black plays here first, as in Dia. 10, he cannot make much territory. White can press him with *2* to 8 and then he has the hane at *a*.

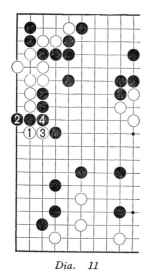

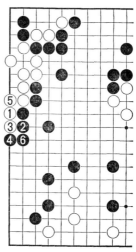

Dia. 11   Dia. 12

C (2 points). White 1 in Dia. 11 does not work. After Black 2 and 4, White has merely given Black two prisoners. The right way for White to play here is to make the hane at 1 in Dia. 12.

Problem	1	2	3	4	5	6	7	8	9	Total
Your score										

Total score	52 or less	54–58	60–64	66–70	72–76	78–82	84–88	90
Rank	8 kyu & up	7–6 kyu	5–4 kyu	3–2 kyu	1 kyu 1 dan	2–3 dan	4–5 dan	6 dan

CHAPTER 5

Games

In this last chapter we shall go through two more of my (Ogawa's) games, and in each of them I have set ten endgame problems for you to try to solve. The first game is one I played in 1967 when I was studying to become a professional at the Kitani Go School. (I believe I was also still attending junior high school.) I had black with a four-stone handicap, and Minoru Kitani, 9-dan, was playing white.

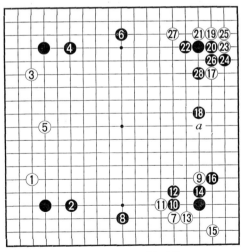

Figure 1 (1—28)

Looking back on this game, I am surprised at how tight and conservative many of my moves were. If I had it to play over again, I would play differently. I would shift Black 4 to 5 in Figure 1, for example, to keep White from getting that ideal 1–3–5 formation, and I would move Black 16 to *a* on the right side. I would move Black 18 to *a*, too. The three-three point invasion at White 19 was obvious, and after Black 28, it would be better to have 18 at *a*, halfway between the black positions above and below, than where it was, too close to the upper position and too far from the lower one. White took advantage of my error by coming in at 29 in Figure 2, and although I attacked and chased him with 30 and so on, he escaped. The impression one gets from the whole opening up through White 47 is that Black has let herself be tricked.

I closed the upper left corner with Black 48, a move that also aimed toward an invasion of the left side, and White responded with the attachment at 49.

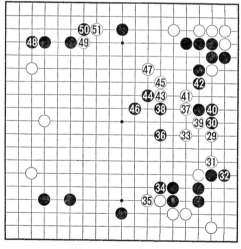

Figure 2 (*29—51*)

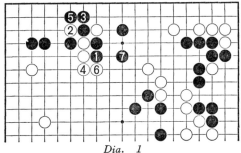

Dia. 1

At Black 54 the standard move is to press on the other side, with Black 1 in Dia. 1. White 2 to Black 7 are a joseki. I cannot recall why I avoided Dia. 1—perhaps I thought it would make the left side too hard to invade—but I leave you to judge the relative merits of it and the sequence through 61 in Figure 3.

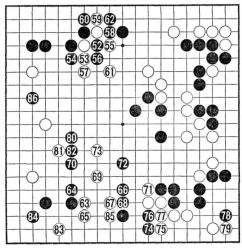

Figure 3 (52—86)

White tried the same type of attachment on the lower side at 63 in Figure 3, and this time I answered by extending to 64 and starting a running fight. White settled himself with 83 to 85, but I had gained the initiative for a promising-looking invasion at 86.

By the end of Figure 4, however, my invasion had turned into a big failure. I had made only a few points of territory on the left side, and had gotten one of my own big groups into eye trouble. One reason for this was my hane at 90; I should just have extended forward to 95. I must have been expecting White to answer Black 98 by connecting the ko at 1 in Dia. 2, after which I could take a thirty-point territory with Black 2, 4, and 6, but Kitani upset my plans by playing White 99 and 101, forcing me to take and connect the ko. With 103 his stones had gotten neatly out into the center, and mine were jammed against the left edge.

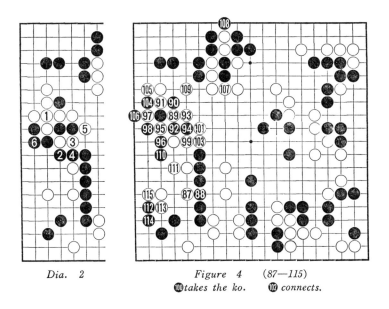

Dia. 2

Figure 4 (87—115)
⑩ *takes the ko.* ⑩ *connects.*

I could have still gotten a good result out of the fighting on the left side if, after White 103 on the last page, I had played Black 1 and 3 in Dia. 3 instead of cutting at *a*. If White used 2 to forestall Black 3, I could play 2 myself and either way I would capture a large area.

Having missed this chance, I was now in a very cramped position. I tried to run my big group out to safety with Black 16 and so on in Figure 5, but the road closed on me at White 43. I had to abandon Black 34, 40, and 42 in the center and go back to the lower left corner to make two eyes. I managed to live with Black 44 in Figure 6, but White forced me with 45, 47, and 49, then tied all his loose groups together by capturing four of my stones in the center with 51. This last move marked the beginning of a grim endgame for me. By now my original advantage from the handicap stones was more than all gone.

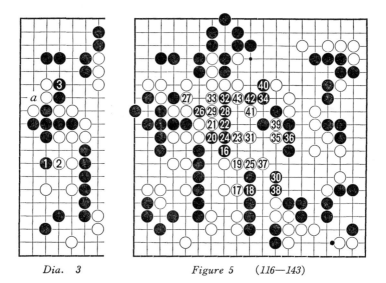

Dia. 3   Figure 5   (116—143)

Actually, I would not have survived even this far if White 49 had not let me take the key defensive point at 50. White 49 looks like a good move—next White can invade the corner at *a*—but if Kitani had played 1, 3, and 5 in Dia. 4 instead, he could have ended the game directly. I would have had to connect at 4 to keep my eyeless center stones from being detached, but then White 7 wouid have killed my left side group.

Anyway, after 52, 54, and 56, I turned to the lower right, where both the black and white positions were weak, and that gives us our first problem.

Problem 1. What is the best way for Black to play in the lower right: *A*, *B*, or *C*? Mark down your choice, then turn the page and read on. The answers are numbered 1, 2, and 3—3 for the best, 1 for the worst—so you can score yourself by giving yourself 1, 2, or 3 points accordingly.

Your choice

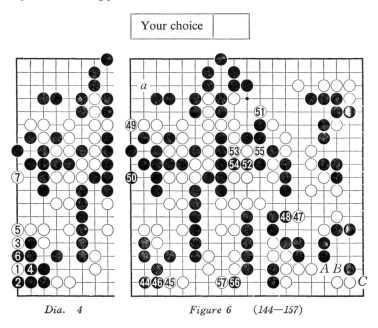

Dia. 4   Figure 6   (144—157)

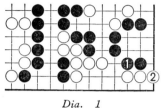

Dia. 1   Dia. 2

1. *B.* Black 1 in Dia. 1 lets White get ample eye space and territory by extending to the key point 2.

2. *A.* Black 1 in Dia. 2 is a bit better, provided that Black follows with the hane at 3, but the 1–2 exchange gives White a simple life with 4. Black 1 is the kind of forcing move that should be left unplayed just on principle.

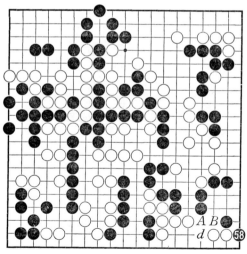

Figure 7   (*158*)

3.   *C*.   The correct move is to start with the hane at 58 in Figure 7.
Now it is not so obvious that White can live, for Black is holding in
reserve not only the push down at *A*, but the attachment at *d* and all
sorts of placement attacks as well.

White did manage to live, with 59 and 61 in Figure 8, but there was
some bad potential left for him.   See if you can read the situation out.

Next I defended the upper left corner, to keep White from invading
with 1 and 3 in Dia. 3.   White 3 in Dia. 3 is correct and damaging
enough, but I may also have been worried about White 3 and 5 in
Dia. 4; although they do not work, anyone who can prove that to
himself quickly is quite strong.

Problem 2.   What is the best way for Black to defend the corner:
A, *B*, or *C*?

Your choice	

Dia.   3

Dia.   4

Figure 8   (*159—161*)

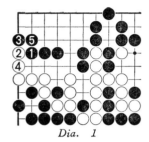

Dia. 1

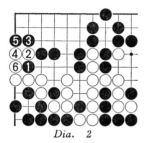

Dia. 2

1. *B.* Black 1 in Dia. 1 is the worst move because it lets White play 2 and 4 in sente.

2. *C.* Black 1 in Dia. 2 is better. It gives White the wedging tesuji at 2, but now White 2 etc. are gote, and therefore less profitable to White, even though they leave Black 1 in atari.

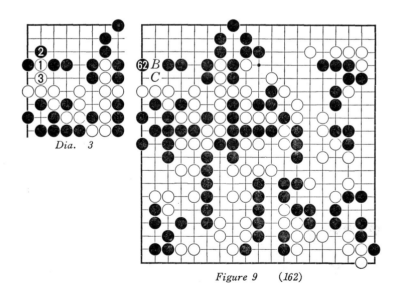

Dia. 3

Figure 9   (*162*)

3. *A*. Black 62 in Figure 9 is correct. White's move—the wedge at 1 in Dia. 3—is again gote, and after 3 there is no black stone left in atari as there was in Dia. 2.

In fact, since White gave atari at 63 in Figure 10, he lost even the possibility of Dia. 3. Now I could answer the wedge with 2 and 4 in Dia. 4, trapping him in a shortage of liberties. This was a slight piece of carelessness by Kitani; he should have exchanged 1 for 2 in Dia. 5 and then given atari at 3, with the connection at *a* left as a possible three-point move for later on.

White 69 was another mistake—it would have been better just to capture at 71—but White's overall idea of taking away my eye on the lower edge was of course correct. By threatening to kill my big group in the lower right he was making profit in sente.

Problem 3. How should Black defend her group—with *A*, *B*, or *C*?

> Your choice

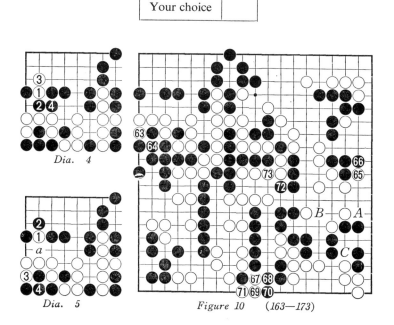

Dia. 4

Dia. 5

Figure 10   (163—173)

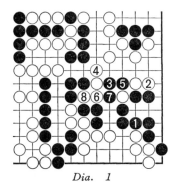

Dia. 1

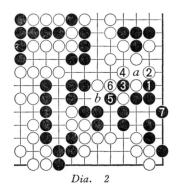

Dia. 2

1. *C.* Black 1 in Dia. 1 is no defense at all. White 2 leaves Black with only one eye, and although she can make a second one with 3 and 5, she has to give up the larger half of her group when White plays 6.

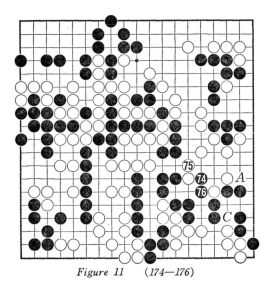

Figure 11 (*174—176*)

2. *A.* Black 1 in Dia. 2 is much better, but White answers the double atari at 3 with 4 and 6, and if Black tries to live by fighting the ko at *a*, White has plenty of big ko threats. Fortunately Black can live unconditionally with 7, but the value of 1, 3, and 5 is likely to be nullified by White's playing *b* in sente, then taking the ko below 3 and putting Black 5 into atari.

3. *B.* Black 74 in Figure 11 is correct. By starting with this move Black can run all the way through White's territory in the lower right center before having to make two eyes on the right side. You should not have much trouble seeing that the sequence through 84 in Figure 12 is better for Black than Dia. 2.

Problem 4. After a forcing move at 85, White turned to the last large area, on the upper side. What is the right extension for him to make there: *A, B,* or *C*?

Your choice	

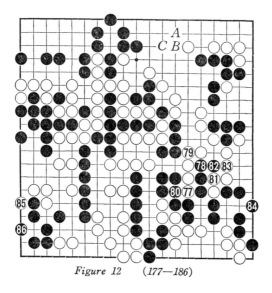

Figure 12   (*177—186*)

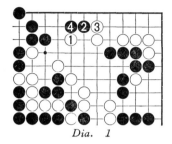

Dia. 1

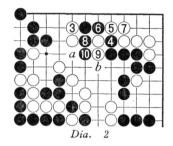

Dia. 2

1. *C.* White 1 in Dia. 1 goes too far. Black can invade behind it at 2, and the whole exchange through 3 and 4 is more profitable to him than to White. If White tries to play as in Dia. 2, Black pushes through at 4, cuts at 6, and comes out with 8 and 10, leaving *a* and *b* as miai.

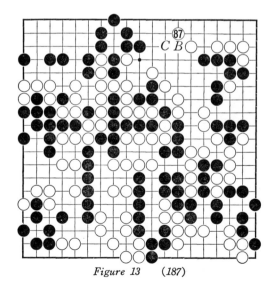

Figure 13   (*187*)

2. *B*. White 1 in Dia. 3 only invites the 2–3 exchange, which leaves White with a glaringly bad empty triangle.

3. *A*. The correct move here is the diagonal extension on the second line in Figure 13. This is also the point that Black would like to take if given the chance.

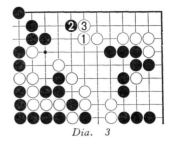

Dia. 3

Having sente again, I made two small forcing moves at 88 and 90 in Figure 14. The first of these was all right, but the second would have been better left unplayed.

Problem 5. Now it is Black's turn for a large gote move. Which of *A*, *B*, and *C* in Figure 14 would be best?

Your choice	

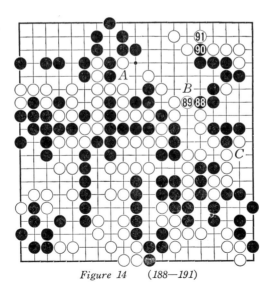

Figure 14   *(188—191)*

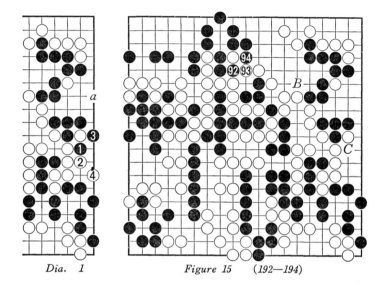

Dia. 1

Figure 15   (192—194)

1. *C.* Black 1 in Dia. 1 is a belladonna move—attractive-looking, but deadly.   If Black captures at 3, White 4 kills her big group in the lower right.   If Black catches herself in time to play 3 at 4, White will capture Black 1, and then Black will have to watch out for a white placement at *a*.

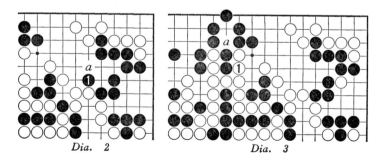

Dia. 2   Dia. 3

2. *B.* At least Black 1 in Dia. 2 causes Black no loss, but it gains her very little. Imagine White answering it at *a*, for example, and you will see how small it is.

3. *A.* Black 92 and 94 in Figure 15 are worth a good five points. Compare them with White 1 in Dia. 3. If Black connects at *a* there, White has gained three points in sente; if Black does not play *a* and White does later, that is another four points. That makes White 1 worth $3+(\frac{1}{2}\times4)=5$ points in gote, and likewise Black 92 and 94. These moves take on some added value, too, in the form of thickness.

Problem 6. White's next move was 95 in Figure 16, which forced Black to connect at 96 to live. Which would be best for White 97: *A, B,* or *C*?

Your choice	

Figure 16   (*195—196*)

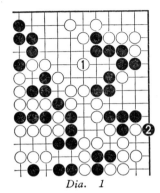

Dia. 1

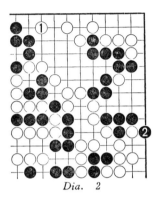

Dia. 2

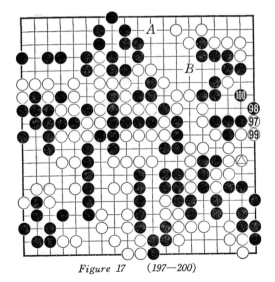

Figure 17　　(197—200)

1. *B.* White 1 in Dia. 1 is not very big, and Black will give atari at 2.

2. *A.* White 1 in Dia. 2 is bigger, being worth a good five points, but Black will still give atari at 2.

3. *C.* White 97 and 99 in Figure 17 are sente, and they reduce Black's territory while enlarging White's. Once White has committed himself by playing 95 (⬳), he cannot afford to delay 97 and 99.

Problem 7. Before taking the large point on the upper side (1 in Dia. 2), White decided to try something on the left side. He started by exchanging 1 for 2 in Figure 18. What is his best continuation: *A*, *B*, or *C*?

Your choice	

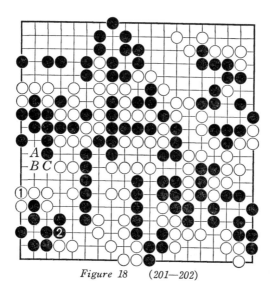

Figure 18 (201—202)

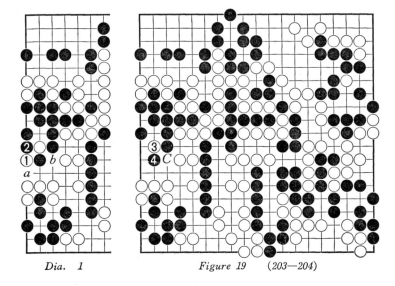

Dia. 1   Figure 19   (203—204)

1. *A*. Kitani actually played the worst move, White 3 in Figure 19. This mistake cost him about four points. He must have thought that he could kill my group by continuing with White 1 in Dia. 1, but Black 2, making *a* and *b* miai, would take care of that.

2. *C*. White 1 and 3 in Dia. 2 on the facing page reduce Black's group to the minimum of three points, (counting one prisoner at ⬤), but White cannot expect to make any territory for himself this way.

3. *B*. White 1 in Dia. 3 reduces Black's group by the same amount, and now White can get two or three points of territory by connecting at *a*, or two points by descending to *c* after Black *a*, White *b*. Black cannot necessarily prevent that by playing *a*, White *b*, Black *c* in sente because White can resist in ko with *d*.

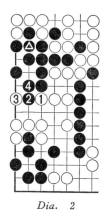

Dia. 2

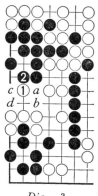

Dia. 3

Problem 8. After White 5 and Black 6 to 12 in Figure 20 it is high time to see what can be done in the lower right corner. Black to play: *A, B,* or *C*?

Your choice	

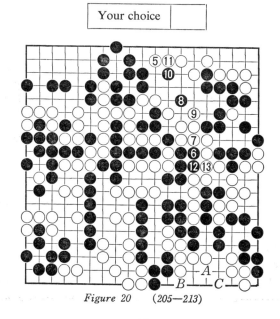

Figure 20   (*205—213*)

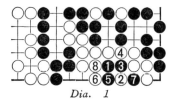

Dia. 1

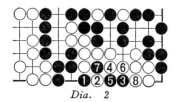

Dia. 2

1. *A.* Black 1 in Dia. 1 would only work if White had no outside liberties. White takes the key point at 2, then squeezes Black with 4, 6 and 8 to live with seven points of territory.

2. *B.* Black 1 and 3 in Dia. 2 are a tesuji combination that will often produce a ko, but here they fail. (Black 3 at 5 would also fail, White answering at 3 or 4). Again White squeezes Black with 6 and 8, and if Black connects at 9 in Dia. 3, White captures at 10. Black cannot make a killing return play at 9 because his four stones to the left are in atari.

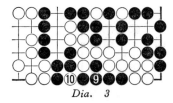

Dia. 3

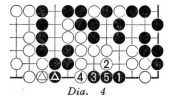

Dia. 4

3. *C.* Black 1 in Dia. 4 leads quite directly to a seki. It is worth noting, incidentally, that this possibility would not have existed if White had not forced the ◇—◆ exchange earlier in the game, since without it White 4 would threaten to link up to the group to the left.

As you can see from Figure 21, I somehow missed the seki in Dia. 4 and made the relatively worthless cut at 14 instead. White lost no time in descending to 15 and getting six points of territory where I could have reduced him to nothing.   If I had played Dia. 4, I would have had a comfortable win.   The score would have stood something like:

Black		White	
Upper left	25	Center and	
Left side	5	right side	17
Lower left	4	Upper right	14
Upper right	7	Lower side	8
Lower right	2	Lower right	0
Total	43	Total	39

When I missed Dia. 4, the game became very close.   Perhaps I was expecting Black 18 to be answered at *d*, but Kitani corrected that notion with White 21.

Problem 9.   How should Black answer White 27 in Figure 21:   at *A*, *B*, or *C*?

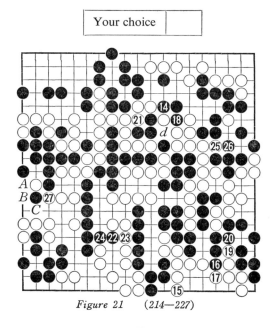

Figure 21   (214—227)

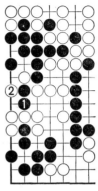

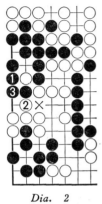

Dia. 1   Dia. 2

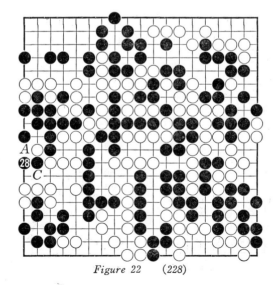

Figure 22   (228)

1. *C.* Black 1 in Dia. 1 is a tragic mistake. White 2 kills the black group.

2. *A.* Black 1 in Dia. 2 is unnecessarily cautious. It lets White give atari with 2 and make one point of territory, at ×, in sente.

3. *B.* Black 28 in Figure 22 is correct. White no longer has that point of territory in sente that he had in Dia. 2. To look at it another way, if White plays *C* later on, there will be no need for Black to reply at *A*.

Problem 10. White's next move was 29 in Figure 23. Choose Black's response from among *A*, *B*, and *C*.

Your choice	

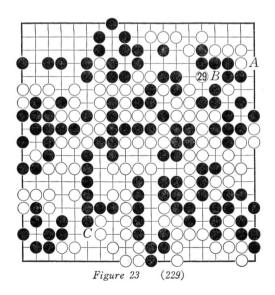

Figure 23   (229)

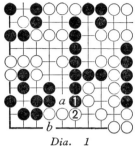

Dia. 1

1. *C.* Black 1 in Dia. 1 actually causes Black a loss. The proper way for her to play here is to sacrifice a stone at 2, followed by White 1, Black *a*, etc., or, equivalently, to hane at *b*.

2. *B.* Black 1 in Dia. 2 gains one point. If White cut at 1, Black would later have to fill at *a*.

3. *A.* Black 30 and 32 in Figure 24 gain two points. They, and Black 1 in Dia. 2, are reverse sente plays, for if Black ignores this part of the board completely, as in Dia. 3, White can gain two points with

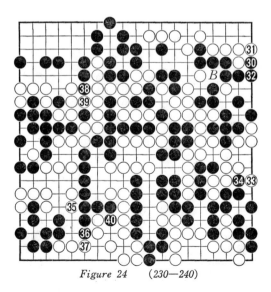

Figure 24   (230—240)

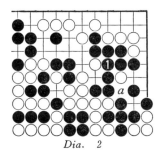

Dia. 2

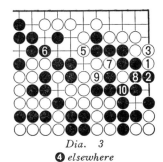

Dia. 3

● elsewhere

1 and 3, then two more points in sente with 5, 7, and 9, and by this stage of the game two points in sente are bigger than anything else.

After Black 30 to 34 on the right side, White used sente to play 35 in Figure 24, forcing me into the undesirable exchange of 36 for 37. At least Black 36 raised the value of Black 40, so that White came back to answer it at 43 in Figure 25, (one point in reverse sente). Black 44 was also worth one point in reverse sente, and thus equal in value to White 45 (two points in gote).

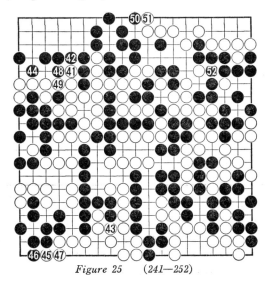

Figure 25   (241—252)

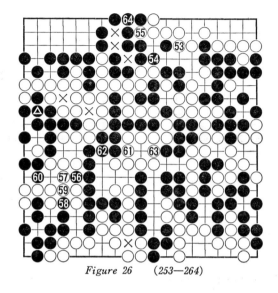

Figure 26   (*253—264*)

White played 53 in Figure 26 in sente, then took the largest remaining point at 55. Black 56 to 60 and White 61 to 63 were miai; each being worth one point in gote, and Black 64 finished the game. Prisoners had been captured at the points marked × and ⬢, making the final score:

Black		White	
Upper left	26	Center and	
Left side	5	right side	16
Lower left	3	Upper right	13
Upper right	7	Lower side	7
Lower right	2	Lower right	6
Total	43	Total	42

I had won by one point. The reason that I set no problems on the last thirty-five moves is that in most cases where there were alternative moves to consider, the alternative move would have led to the same final score as the move actually played.

I was badly outdone in the opening and middle game, and even though Kitani missed the finishing blow at White 149 (Figure 6), I went into the endgame behind. I should have lost, but a number of un-Kitani-like errors let me catch up and go ahead. I made one major oversight toward the end, missing the seki in the lower right corner, but fortunately it was not quite enough to cost me the lead.

Most of the problems in this game were tesuji problems, and it is interesting to observe that none of them exactly matched the standard tesuji that appeared in chapter three. This illustrates the fact that every game generates its own unique positions, and you have to try to read them out and hunt for the right plays on your own. Now score youself.

Game 1

Problem	1	2	3	4	5	6	7	8	9	10	Total
Your score											

Perfect score: 30

In the next game the stress will be less on tesuji and more on judging the relative merits of various moves in different parts of the board. I think you will find the problems more difficult. Some of them call for considerable reading, so take your time. The game is one I played recently against Yutaka Ono, 4-dan, in the preliminary rounds of the Meijin tournament. Again I had black, but this time, of course, there was no handicap, and to make the game exactly even there was a $5\frac{1}{2}$-point komi, that is, the final score would be adjusted $5\frac{1}{2}$ points in White's favor to compensate for Black's having the first move. To win, therefore, I would have to finish at least six points ahead on the board. As you will see, neither player was able to open up a big lead in the opening or middle game, so the issue was left to be decided in the endgame.

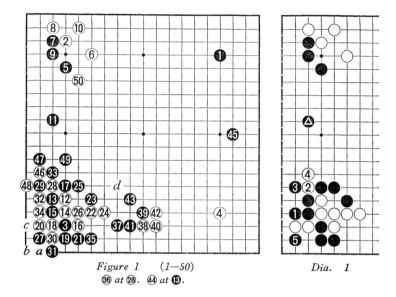

Figure 1   (1—50)

㊱ at ㉘. ㊹ at ⑬.

Dia. 1

The fighting in this game started early, with a difficult variation of the small avalanche joseki in the lower left corner. Since 28 to 34 gave White three liberties, I had to crawl out at 35 and let him capture my cutting stones with 36. The cause of this was Black 27, which I should have played at 1 in Dia. 1. The standard sequence there is bad for White because the stone marked ❷ is blocking his development. During the game I was worried about his playing 2 in Dia. 2 on the facing page before cutting—after White 10 there I lose my stones on the lower side in a ko—but I was overlooking the descending tesuji at 5 in Dia. 3.

White 46 was a double sente point. I would have liked to play there and have White answer by living with *a*, Black *b*, White *c*, but he could hold *a–b–c* in reserve and come out at *d*, and I did not want to encourage that. Anyway, for future counting purposes, remember that White has captured three stones in the lower left corner and Black has captured one.

— 190 —

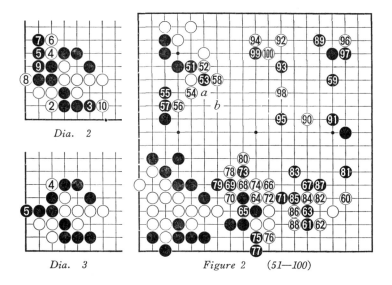

Dia. 2

Dia. 3

Figure 2   (51—100)

The fighting continued in Figure 2. Since White 58 captured Black 53 without recourse to a ladder, (Black *a*, White *b*), I should have played Black 57 at 58. Still, by exchanging with Black 83 to 87 to form a large area on the right side and attacking in the center with Black 93 and 95, I was holding my own in the game.

Problem 1. The black group on the lower side has become isolated. If White attacks it with 1 in the diagram below, should Black respond at *A*, *B*, or *C*? This is a life-and-death question, but it is related to the endgame.

Your choice	

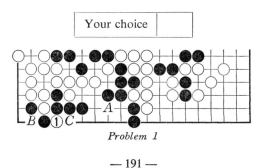

Problem 1

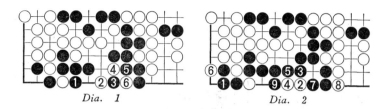

Dia. 1   Dia. 2

1. *C.* Capturing at 1 in Dia. 1 allows White to force a ko fight for the life of the whole group.

2. *B.* In the first place, if White answered Black 1 in Dia. 2 directly at 6, Black would have accomplished nothing. White has an even better opportunity, however, in 2 and 4. Black must answer at 3 and 5, and then White can play both 6 and 8 in sente. Black lives, but three of his stones are left hanging and the lower edge is sealed off.

3. *A.* Dia. 3 on the facing page shows the best defense. Two black stones are still left hanging, but now if White plays 1 in Dia. 4

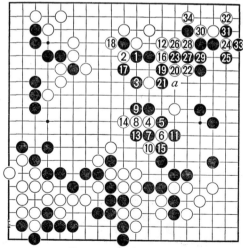

Figure 3   (*101—134*)

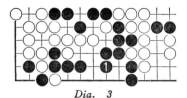

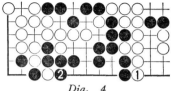

Dia. 3   Dia. 4

Black can reply with 2, so White cannot both seal off the lower edge and retain the option of capturing the corner, as he did in Dia. 2.

Figure 3 brought the middle game to a close, and although I made a mistake at 21, which I should have played at *a*, and White was able to gouge out my upper right corner, I was, if anything, very slightly ahead, considering that I had the next move.

Problem 2. Black to play and start the endgame. Which is best: *A, B,* or *C*?

Your choice	

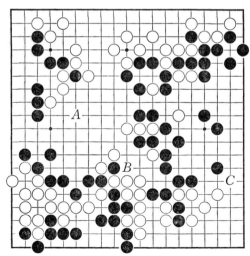

Problem 2

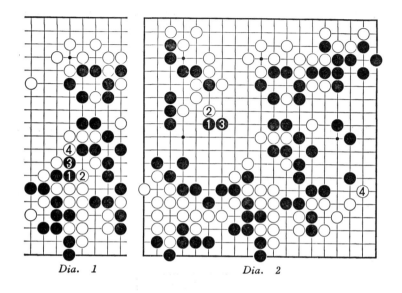

Dia. 1   Dia. 2

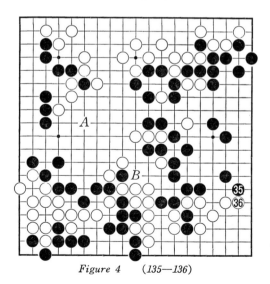

Figure 4   (135—136)

1. *B.* This is a blunder. As Dia. 1 shows, it ends in a shortage of liberties for Black.

2. *A.* White will answer Black 1 in Dia. 2 with 2, but then Black has to continue with 3, which is clearly gote, and White gets to take the important double sente point at 4. Black 1 is not really the best move for Black in the center anyway.

3. *C.* Black 35 in Figure 4 would have been sente for either side now, so I took it without delay. The center was, by comparison, a relatively neutral area.

Problem 3. For the next few problems you will be putting yourself in White's place. To start with, how would you answer Black 37 in the figure below on the lower edge: at *A*, *B*, or *C*?

Your choice	

Figure 5   (*137*)

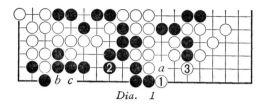

Dia. 1

1.   *C.*   By blocking at 1 in Dia. 1 White can make Black defend at 2, but then he has to defend himself against Black *a* by playing 3, and he has lost the opportunity he had to capture the two black stones in the corner by cutting at *b*.   If he cuts at *b* after Black 2, Black can answer with *c*.

2.   *A.*   It is better for White to draw back with 1 in Dia. 2 on the facing page in order to preserve the possibility of capturing the two stones in the corner.   This also, however, leaves Black the possibility of descending to *a* at some time in the future and forcing White to use extra moves capturing him.

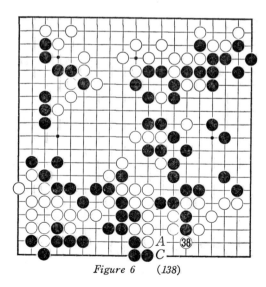

Figure 6   (*138*)

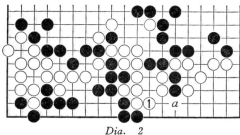

Dia. 2

3. *B.* It is best to drop all the way back to White 38 in Figure 6, immobilizing the two black prisoners there. White need not worry about losing territory on the lower edge, since he can always play *C* in sente and anything Black did there would be gote.

Problem 4. After playing 39 and 41 in Figure 7 in sente, I pushed out at 43. White to play: *A*, *B*, or *C*?

Your choice

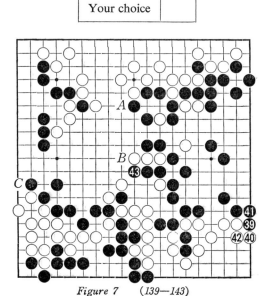

Figure 7 (*139—143*)

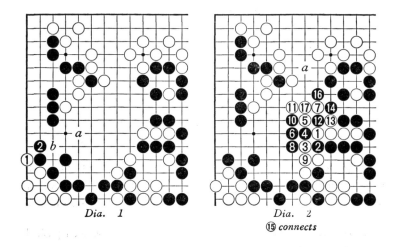

Dia. 1

Dia. 2

⑮ *connects*

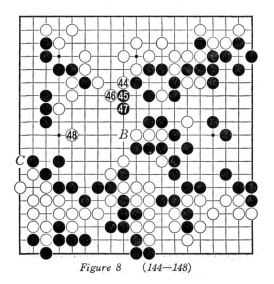

Figure 8 (144—148)

1. *C.* The exchange in Dia. 1 only helps Black by removing the possibility of a white peeping move at *b* or clamp at 2. It would be better for White to extend to *a* and aim towards those possibilities from the center. 1 will still be his sente later if he wants it, while a black descent to 1 would be gote.

2. *B.* Black will push through and cut at 2 and 4 in Dia. 2 and force White through the sequence shown. This costs White a great deal; he can no longer get into the lower left center area, and Black can barge into his territory at *a*. Saving the three white stones is not worth it.

3. *A.* White 44 and 46 in Figure 8 are sente, and compared with a black play at 44, they are quite large. If Black omits 45 or 47, White can give atari to the right of or below 45 and take the lion's share of the center. White 48 makes a good continuation.

Problem 5. I retaliated in the center with 49 in Figure 9, and White used his next move to attack my group on the lower side. Did he play *A, B,* or *C*?

Your choice	

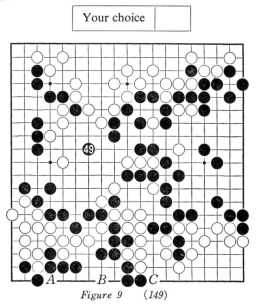

Figure 9 (*149*)

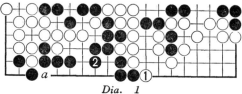

Dia. 1

1. *C.* If White plays 1 in Dia. 1 Black defends at 2, and White has lost the possibility of capturing the two black stones in the corner with *a*, as has already been explained twice.

2. *A.* White 1 in Dia. 2 on the facing page is answered by the same Black 2, and although White can capture the corner, Black can return the favor by pushing out at *a*, or if White plays *a*, Black can capture White 1.

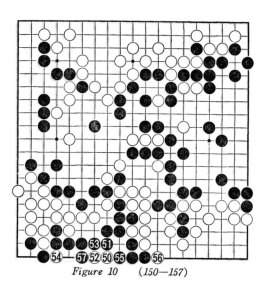

Figure 10   (*150—157*)

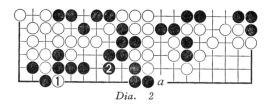

Dia. 2

3. *B.* White 50 in Figure 10 is a tesuji that enables White both to block at 56 in sente and to leave the two corner stones vulnerable to capture. In other words, White now has the possibility of getting both plays, while in Dias. 1 and 2 he could get only one. Black's territory is five or six points in the figure, six points in Dia. 1, and about five points (an average value) in Dia. 2, so the sacrifice of 50 and 52 does not make Black's territory any bigger.

Problem 6. What about White's next move: *A*, *B*, or *C*?

Your choice	

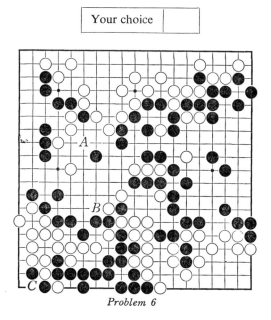

Problem 6

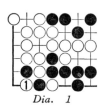

Dia. 1

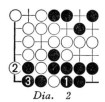

Dia. 2

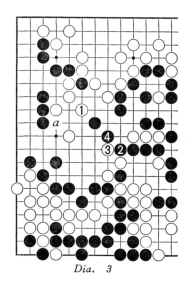

Dia. 3

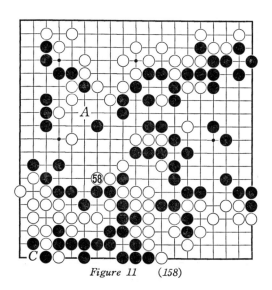

Figure 11 (*158*)

1. *C.* Capturing these two stones is worth exactly seven points in gote; compare Dias. 1 and 2 and you will see that there is a difference of six points of white territory and one white prisoner. There are bigger gote moves elsewhere.

2. *A.* White 1 in Dia. 3, stopping a black play there, is big, but too passive. It gives Black a good excuse to play 2 and 4. If White is going to defend here, White *a*, in sente, would be better.

3. *B.* White 58 in Figure 11 is a reverse sente move, since White would have to respond to a black atari at 58, and the difference between White 58 and Black 58 is not small.

Problem 7. Since White had ignored Black ⬤, I kept on with 59 and 61, threatening to draw my stone out at *a* and capture the whole center. White 62 restored the shortage of liberties that had been preventing Black *a* earlier, (now if Black plays *a*, White gives atari above *a*, then from the right), and Black 63 left an interesting position. Should White's next move be *A*, *B*, or *C*?

Your choice	

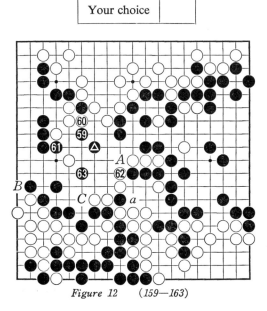

Figure 12   (*159—163*)

— 203 —

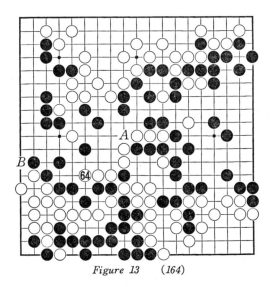

Figure 13   (*164*)

1. *B.* It is still too early for this hane. White still has other potential here that he should keep open.

2. *A.* Although worth eight points at the very least, this connection would be gote. That sets it apart from the next move.

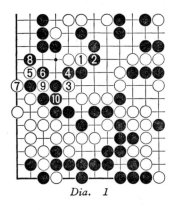

Dia. 1

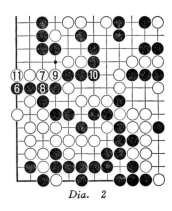

Dia. 2

3. *C.* White 64 in Figure 13 is large in itself, and it conceals an even larger threat. If Black ignores it, White can play 1 and 3 in Dia. 1, then clamp at 5. Black has to answer this at 6 and let White make a tidy profit in sente with 7 and 9. If he tries to cut White off with 6 etc. in Dia. 2, he loses a big group of stones, being behind, four liberties to three.

When you consider that after 64 White can push into the space below it and capture two stones, and that White 64 destroys three or four points of territory that Black could make by playing there, you can easily appreciate its value.

Problem 8. Since Dia. 1 would have been both large and sente for White, I defended at 65 in the figure below, and now that he finally had no other possibilities to save on the left edge, he played 66. His connection at 68 left me a choice of three big points around the edges: *A*, *B*, and *C*. Which was the biggest?

Your choice	

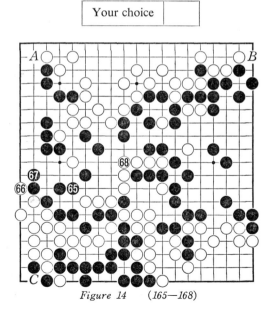

Figure 14   *(165—168)*

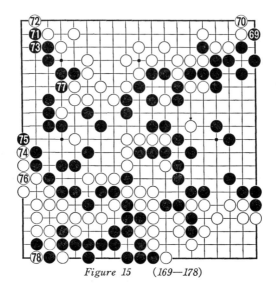

Figure 15   (*169—178*)

1. *C*. (78 in Figure 15). As we saw before, this move is worth only seven points in gote.

2. *A*. (71 in Figure 15). If you compare the figure with Dia. 1, where *a* is White's sente, you will find a difference of 4 points of white territory and 5(−) points of black territory, making this a 9(−)-point gote play. There is also the possibility of White's descending to 1 in Dia. 2. If Black answers, White has gained about four points in sente, and if Black does not answer, White can play the monkey jump in Dia.

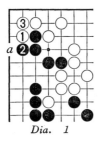

Dia. *1*

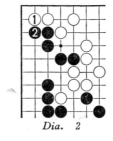

Dia. *2*

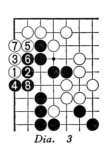

Dia. *3*

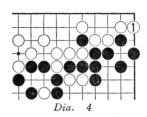

Dia. 4

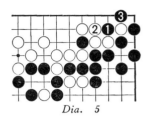

Dia. 5

3. Dias. 1 and 3 should be devalued slightly because they reduce the effectiveness of White 74 in the figure.

3. *B.* (69 in Figure 15). This play only gains four points as compared with White 1 in Dia. 4, but it threatens the eight-point capture shown in Dia. 5. That makes it sente; Black can play it and, White 70 and 73 being about equal, White has nothing better to do than answer. Note that the sequence Black 69, White 71, Black 73, White 70 would leave Black with sente to take 78.

Problem 9. I took the iast large point at 79 in Figure 16. Should White's next play be *A*, *B*, or *C*?

Your choice	

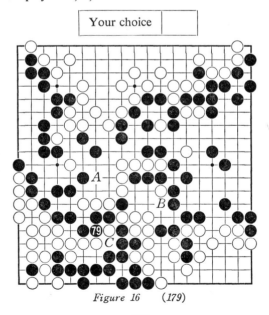

Figure 16 (*179*)

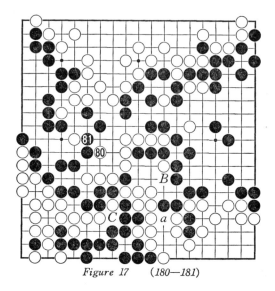

Figure 17   *(180—181)*

1. *C.* This is a mere two points in gote.

2. *B.* This move is worth four points. If Black plays 1 in **Dia.** 1, she gets two points for taking the prisoner, one for not having to connect at ×, and another because she can push down at *a* in sente, whereas after White *B* in the figure, *a* would be White's sente.

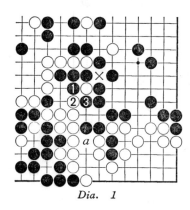

Dia. 1

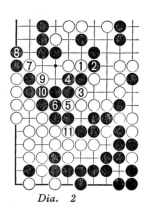

Dia. 2

3. *A.* White 80 in Figure 17 is worth about three points, but unlike White *B*, it is sente. If Black does not reply, White 1 to 11 in Dia. 2 end the game.

Problem 10. White made sente plays at 82 and 84 in Figure 18, then cut at 86 and pushed all the way down the edge to 96. He played 86 to 96 to keep me from answering 98 at 96, so that later on he could gain another point by playing *a*. Of course he did not lose anything except possible ko threats by filling my territory with prisoners in this way.

White 104 was the last move worth more than two points, and now, taking into account that Black's turn is next, can you tell how the score stands? Try to work out the rest of the endgame in your head, or on the board if you have been laying the moves out on one, and see if you think:

A. Black has a clear lead, (1½ points or more).

B. The game will be decided by half a point.

C. White has a clear lead.

Don't forget the 5½-point komi.

Your
opinion

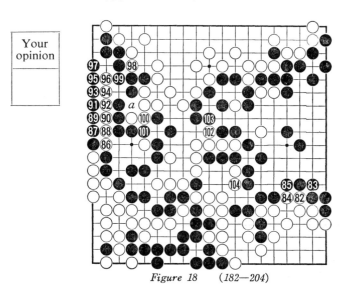

Figure 18   (*182—204*)

— 209 —

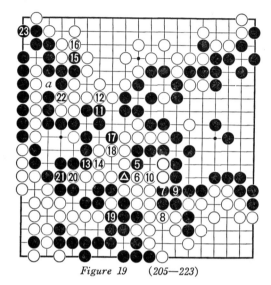

Figure 19   (205—223)

Black 5 to 9 kept White from making any extra territory at 6 or 10, and Black 11 turned out to be sente, since it was worth a good two points for White to defend at 12. White's defending moves at 14 and 18 were also worth two points, keeping ⬤ from being a false eye, and I took the last two-point play at 19. White 20 and 22 were worth one point each, (eventually I would have to connect at *a*), and Black 23 finished the game. This whole sequence was more or less unavoidable. Compare your counting with the following:

White		Black	
Center and lower right	29	Left side	23
Upper side	44	Right side	58
Lower left	12	Lower side	7
Total	85	Total	88

I was ahead by three points on the board, but with the komi, I had lost by two and a half.

This had been a difficult endgame, marked by a fair amount of trading back and forth in the center. When I went over it again at home I think I found one or two ways I could have won by playing differently, but it is the moves you actually make, not the ones you discover the next day, that count. I would prefer to forgo a post-mortem analysis.

Score yourself on the ten problems of this game, then add together your totals from the two games of this chapter and compare the result with the chart below to get some idea of your level of skill. No claim is made for the accuracy of this rating, or the ones you received in chapters two and four. For one thing, it is easier to exercise good judgement when working out problems in a book than when caught up in the heat of actual play. For another thing, in actual play you have no A–B–C hints to guide you. Finally, the end-game is only one part of the game; you may be strong at it but weak in the opening, for example, or vice versa.

Game 2

Problem	1	2	3	4	5	6	7	8	9	10	Total
Your score											

Perfect score: 30

Total Score: Game 1 + Game 2

Less than 40	40	42	44	46	48	50	52	54	56	58	60
6 kyu or above	5 kyu	4	3	2	1 kyu	1 dan	2	3	4	5	6 dan

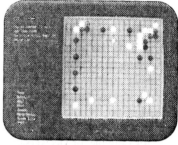

Books and Playing Sets for Chinese Chess, Shogi and GO

Whenever you're looking for the best in strategy games from the Orient, think of Ishi Press. We're committed to offering English-speaking readers the best in all these fascinating games.

We offer an excellent introductory books on Chinese Chess (*Xiangqi*) and Japanese Chess (*Shogi*). Subscribe to our new quarterly newsletter about Shogi, *Shogi World,* just $9 a year in the US, $12 in Canada, and $14 in other countries.

The other classical game of strategy from the Orient is GO (*Weichi* in Chinese or *Pahduk* in Korean). We publish the most complete collection of books about GO to be found in any Western language. We also publish *GO World*, the definitive GO magazine of the English-speaking world. Subscriptions to *GO World* are $15 a year in the US and $18 in Canada.

We offer the most complete selection of GO-playing equipment to be found anywhere in the western world. Whether you are looking for a basic set with glass stones and a folding board or the most elegant traditional GO board with slate and clamshell stones in polished wooden bowls, we've got it.

We also carry a selection of Shogi sets with both traditional and international-style playing pieces and a good-quality Chinese Chess set with durable plastic chessmen and a folding wood board.

Ask your local retailer for Ishi Press books and games or send for our free catalog

Books about GO
from Ishi Press

BEGINNER BOOKS

AN INTRODUCTION TO GO
   by James Davies and Richard Bozulich
THE MAGIC OF GO
   by Cho Chikun

ELEMENTARY BOOKS

THE SECOND BOOK OF GO
   by Richard Bozulich
BASIC TECHNIQUES OF GO
   by Haruyama Isamu and Nagahara Yoshiaki
LESSONS IN THE FUNDAMENTALS OF GO
   by Kageyama Toshiro

Elementary Go Series

VOLUME 1: IN THE BEGINNING
   by Ishigure Ikuro
VOLUME 2: 38 BASIC JOSEKI
   by Kosugi Kiyoshi and James Davies
VOLUME 3: TESUJI
   by James Davies
VOLUME 4: LIFE AND DEATH
   by James Davies
VOLUME 5: ATTACK AND DEFENSE
   by Ishida Akira and James Davies

VOLUME 6: THE ENDGAME
  by Ogawa Tomoko and James Davies
VOLUME 7: HANDICAP GO
  by Nagahara Yoshiaki and Richard Bozulich

INTERMEDIATE BOOKS

STRATEGIC CONCEPTS OF GO
  by Nagahara Yoshiaki
THE BREAKTHROUGH TO SHO-DAN
  by Miyamoto Naoki
KATO'S ATTACK AND KILL
  by Kato Masao
THE DIRECTION OF PLAY
  by Kajiwara Takeo
THE POWER OF THE STAR-POINT
  by Takagawa Shukaku
THE CHINESE OPENING
  Kato Masao
POSITIONAL JUDGMENT
  by Cho Chikun

ADVANCED BOOKS

DICTIONARY OF BASIC JOSEKI (3 Volumes)
  by Ishida Yoshio
ENCLOSURE JOSEKIS
  by Takemiya Masaki
REDUCING TERRITORIAL FRAMEWORKS
  by Fujisawa Shuko
INVINCIBLE: THE GAMES OF SHUSAKU
  edited by John Power